3.99

Linda J Reed

WRESTLING
WITH A PENCIL

Wrestling

with a pencil

The Life of a Freelance Artist
NORMAN THELWELL

Methuen London

First published in 1986
by Methuen London Ltd
11 New Fetter Lane, London EC4P 4EE
Text and illustrations Copyright © Norman Thelwell 1986

Made and printed in Great Britain

The drawings on pages 21, 122, 126, 127, 132, 187 and
190 first appeared in *Punch* and are reproduced by kind
permission of the proprietors.
    The drawing on page 187 first appeared in *The Tatler*
and is reproduced by kind permission of the proprietors.
    The photograph on page 60 is reproduced by kind
permission of the Holburne Museum, Bath.
    The photograph on page 192 is by Mr Brock.

British Library Cataloguing in Publication Data

Thelwell
    Wrestling with a Pencil.
    1. Thelwell   2. Cartoonists – Great Britain
    –Biography
    I. Title
    741'.092'4   NC1479.T54

ISBN 0–413–59320–7

by Norman Thelwell

first published	paperback edition	
1957	1970	Angels on Horseback
1959	1970	Thelwell Country
1960		A Place of Your Own
1961		Thelwell in Orbit
1962	1969	A Leg at Each Corner
1964	1982	Top Dog
1965	1969	Thelwell's Riding Academy
1967	1972	Up the Garden Path
1967	1972	The Compleat Tangler
1970	1974	Thelwell's Book of Leisure
1970	1975	This Desirable Plot
	1970	Thelwell's Horse Box (containing *A Leg at Each Corner*, *Thelwell's Riding Academy*, *Angels on Horseback* and *Gymkhana* paperbacks)
1971	1982	The Effluent Society
	1972	Penelope
	1972	Thelwell's Pony Painting Book
1973	1976	Three Sheets in the Wind
1974	1977	Belt Up
1975	1982	Thelwell Goes West
	1976	Thelwell's Leisure Chest (containing *Up the Garden Path*, *The Compleat Tangler*, *Thelwell's Book of Leisure* and *This Desirable Plot* paperbacks)
1977	1982	Thelwell's Brat Race
1977		Thelwell Frieze
1978	1982	A Plank Bridge By A Pool
	1978	Thelwell's Laughter Case (containing *The Effluent Society*, *Belt Up*, *Three Sheets in the Wind* and *Top Dog* paperbacks)
1979	1982	Thelwell's Gymkhana
1979		Pony Birthday Book
1980		Horse Sense (hardback edition of *Thelwell Frieze*)
1981	1986	Thelwell's Pony Cavalcade (including *Angels on Horseback*, *A Leg at Each Corner* and *Thelwell's Riding Academy*)
1981	1983	A Millstone Round My Neck
1982	1984	Some Damn Fool's Signed The Rubens Again
1983	1985	Thelwell's Magnificat
1984		Thelwell's Sporting Prints

CONTENTS

1: THE DISTANT LANDSCAPE

Eddy's farm, looking across the Wirral towards the River Dee. I spent a lot of time here with friends between leaving school and joining the Army. This sketch was done in August 1940 a few days before the first bombs were dropped in the area.

I don't remember being born, nor anything else until I was somewhere in my third year. No doubt I had conversed with my mother many times before but the first full conversation I can clearly recall took place when my Auntie Margaret was present. They were standing in our kitchen, arms folded, talking about whatever grown-ups talked about.

'What can I draw, Mam?' Either she didn't hear me or she found the question too tedious to deal with at that moment. I pulled at her skirt.

'What can I draw, Mam?'

'Draw a motor car,' she said and went on talking to Auntie.

'I've drawn a motor car . . .'

'Well draw a boat.'

'I've drawn a boat.'

'Draw a house then!'

'I've drawn a house . . .' . . . 'Mam! I've drawn a house.'

'Oh for goodness sake, child! Go and draw yourself.'

It was the first time I had come face to face with a brilliant idea. I went away instantly and made a drawing of myself. I don't remember how long it took me but it was obviously far less time than my mother had hoped. I had to drag at her skirt several times before she looked down. She took my piece of paper, made another point or two to my Auntie, glanced at my drawing and looked stunned. She handed the scrap of paper back to me as if it were hot.

'What did you want to draw yourself doing that for?' she said.

'Let me see, Norm,' said Auntie, taking my self-portrait. She turned her face away instantly making strangled little sobs. I think she was laughing at something.

'Kids!' said my mother. 'Who'd have 'em?'

It was my first lesson in the power of the visual arts.

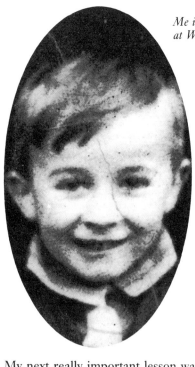

*Me in the five-year-old class
at Well Lane Infants School.*

My next really important lesson was learned shortly after I went to school at five. It had nothing to do with art. I liked Class One. We did a lot of drawing with chalks on brown paper and were allowed, nay encouraged, to mess about with sand and a certain amount of water on large trays.

We were told that there were once people who did not have houses to live in and were forced to live in holes in the ground.

'They were called pit-dwellers,' said Miss Bywaters – 'What were they called?'

'Pit-dwellers, Miss Bywaters,' we all chanted.

'Now I want you all to make pits in the sand today, like the pit-dwellers made to live in.'

Life at school was obviously going to be one long holiday.

I can still recall quite a number of the children from Class One. There were a few who cried from time to time and wanted to go home, but on the whole we were a lively, interested crew. There was Mary Wild who wore black lace-up boots almost up to her knees and kept telling the teacher, and anyone else who would listen, that she could lace them up herself. There was Ben who showed no interest whatever in making homes for pit-dwellers but enjoyed smashing his little red fists into everyone else's architectural efforts. But best of all I remember Frank Smith. He was a bright, sparkling, little comic. Cheerful, likeable and a born life-and-soul-of-the-party. He had an extraordinary vocabulary for his age and words poured from his lips which most of us had never heard before, much less used. He was less skilful with his hands than he was with his mouth and kept dropping sand and spilling water. 'Blast! Me f—ing pit's fallen in again,' he announced. He walked his little fingers across the sand tray making a trail of footprints. 'This is a f—ing pit-dweller looking for a f—ing pit,' he said. He was a bundle of laughs.

My brother, Alan, was nearly two years older than me and a lot bigger. I suppose little Frank had been my hero for a week or more when a domestic fracas occurred in our parlour – which was not uncommon. I had been to Liverpool shopping with my mother and returned with a big orange balloon of the kind which Blackler's stores distributed to the children of their customers. Alan was playing with my balloon and refused to return it to me. I was leaping into the air trying to grab it

*With my mother and elder brother Alan
on a short holiday at Colwyn Bay.
I was two years old at the time.*

*Number 25, Crofton Road, Tranmere, where I was born.
It has not changed much except for
a new front door and a coach lamp.*

but Alan kept flicking it out of my reach. I was
alternately going for his midriff and leaping at the
balloon when the ruckus brought my mother in at
a fast trot.

'Whatever's going on *now*?' she demanded, red
in the face.

'Blast! He won't give me my f—ing balloon,' I
yelled, going for his middle with my head down. I
was still running when my mother hoisted me into
the air by the front of my jersey. At five years old I
had no fillings in my teeth, which was a mercy,
otherwise they would all have shot out during the
shaking I got. What she was saying during my
trauma was a bit confused but I gathered that it
was not the fracas that upset her but something I'd
said. When my head cleared I concluded that
words as well as drawings could have a powerful
effect on grown-ups.

I discovered the magic of colour as soon as I was
big enough to peep through the glass panel of the
lobby door. We lived in a two-up, two-down
terraced house in Birkenhead, Cheshire, which was
organised, cleaned and polished to a sparkle by my

mother, who managed to organise, clean and polish the rest of the family too and handled what money there was about with such care and firmness that she could make a ten-shilling note in her purse do more work than the average pound in anyone else's. The lobby was a wooden cubicle, not much bigger than a telephone kiosk, and its purpose was to keep any draughts that might have the temerity to creep through the front door from entering her parlour. The glass panel was made up of sections of clear, brightly coloured glass which outshone even the kitchen range when the firelight flickered on the Zebro polished metal.

As soon as I was big enough to apply my eye to these enchanted peepholes I discovered another wonder of the world. The view beyond, when the front door was open, was fairly mundane: just the house opposite with a bit of sky above and perhaps the children I knew playing out in the street. But seen through the stained glass it was transformed. Merely by moving my eye from one colour to another I could change the atmosphere, the mood, the weather and – to my surprise – the temperature. The blue glass could make me almost shiver, the yellow bathed the world in bright sunshine, the reds were exotic and exciting, and the greens produced a cool, dream-like effect.

Some years later I read a small booklet on painting and when I came to a bit about hot and cold colours I knew that I had not been the only one to have peeped through a lobby door.

At that stage of my life most of the pictures I saw tended to be either frightening or very sad and I wonder that I was not put off art for life. There was still a tendency for children's books to insist on pressing home a moral and this was invariably backed up by threats of what happened to children who misbehaved. We were sent to Sunday school every week and taught to say our prayers before we went to sleep, but it was all very puzzling. I used to ask Jesus to keep me safe 'till morning light' and was fairly confident that he would; but on the wall by my bed was a picture called 'Jesus in the garden of Gethsemane' which transfixed me with doubt and fear. Poor Jesus was kneeling by a bleak rock

with clasped hands held out in supplication. His face, turned towards heaven, was lit by a jagged bolt of lightning from the black clouds. His clothing was loose and flowing and quite unsuitable for the appalling weather. I wondered how he was going to cope with keeping me safe when he had such problems of his own; and what was worse was the certainty that he knew what I was thinking. There was a picture on the Sunday school wall which showed Jesus surrounded by a multinational crèche of cherubic infants on a nice day. It was called 'Suffer the little children to come unto me'. I got considerable comfort and reassurance from that picture but I worried a bit about the word 'suffer'.

In our living-room was a pair of pictures. (Grown-ups seemed to think of pictures like they thought of boots, trousers or braces: they were better if they came in pairs.) These pictures both showed a cherubic little girl in a white nightie and white floppy bonnet messing about with several cherubic white puppy dogs. One had a pup under her arm and was waving to several others in the top right-hand corner of the picture. It was called 'Bye-bye'. The other picture on the other side of the fireplace showed the same child (or her twin sister) doing much the same thing but she was doing a crouching sort of walk like Groucho Marx and that one was called 'Don't 'e tippie toey' or something very like it. I hated them. They were typical of girls. My antipathy to girls when I was an infant was, happily, very short-lived and stemmed entirely from the fact that boys were not allowed to hit them. It was not that I had the slightest desire to hit them but it seemed grossly unfair that if they hit me, which they often did, I was not allowed to hit back or even to cry. It was a known fact that if a boy, however tiny and innocent, let fall a tear when a girl clouted him he would be ostracised by everyone and have names called after him in the street.

There was another pair of pictures in the parlour – one above the piano and the other over the fireplace – and I found them very disturbing but I didn't know why. One was 'The meeting of

Dante and Beatrice'. This showed a couple of people in long clothes whom I took to be men, standing on a bridge and looking at two other people who I was quite certain were very grown-up ladies. The ladies were striding out in the street, dressed in thin figure-hugging frocks which would have caused a few pursed lips in our street I can tell you. The other one was 'Dante's Dream' and was even more puzzling. A couple of people were holding a bedsheet along the top of the picture while some others were cavorting about underneath it. They didn't seem to be doing anything special and didn't seem to be enjoying it either.

I wanted to ask my mother about those pictures but some instinct told me to leave well alone. If my mother allowed them into her parlour that was all the qualification they needed. Besides, if Beatrice was the one I took to be her, I liked her much better than those namby-pamby kids with the puppies.

Little boys were not expected to retaliate if little girls clouted them.
(From *Brat Race*.)

The other pictures which affected me deeply were contained in a large photograph album. They were lovely and terribly sad. All of them were postcards sent to my mother or my Auntie Margaret by my father and my uncle during the First World War. Most of them were coloured pictures of soldiers, usually alone, sitting by neat little camp-fires or leaning back against a rock or tree and dreaming of the lady who was above their heads surrounded by a dreamy fuzz. All had verses or quotations like 'Just before the battle, mother, I am thinking most of you.' I cried buckets over them and loved every moment of the experience.

I loved the richly embroidered cards, too, emblazoned with crossed flags and wine glasses, and on one even the words 'Entente Cordiale' were worked in glossy silks. They were more exotic than anything I had ever seen in my life and I longed to have just one of them for my very own, particularly one of those in the form of a lace envelope which contained a little card with a message of longing and devotion. But they were 'not for children to play with, just to look at'. I wonder where they all went?

Although I loved drawing things above all else, I had no idea that it would ever be possible for me to earn money by doing it. In the twenties and thirties – in Birkenhead – people didn't talk that kind of nonsense. It was obvious, however, that some people were able to do it and it seemed to me that if their pay was in proportion to the size of their pictures they must be millionaires. For the town was full of hoardings and the hoardings were covered with posters and pictures of all kinds. Huge pictures. Gigantic pictures. There was a fruit pie on the Old Chester Road big enough for a whole family to live in. It was built of Atora beef suet according to the two-feet-high lettering, and the plums which were pouring out of it in a river of crimson juice were bigger than the 'footies' we kicked around Vicky Park. There were men carrying enormous loads with the strength they got from Guinness and rabbits furnishing their homes with chairs and tables they got from . . . I think it was the Times Furnishing Company.

The men who made the pictures put their names on the bottom corner in letters six inches high and three feet wide. There were Tom Purvis, Austin Cooper and many more. I imagined them all living together on a kind of Mount Olympus. They all wore white nightshirts and white beards and held paint brushes ten feet high. When the mood took them they would swing their great brushes and flashes of coloured lightning would crackle from the ends and another mammoth picture would appear on someone's gable-end.

The world was full of wickedness – even then – and if kids could reach the bottom corner of the picture they would take fiendish delight in trying to rip as big a piece as possible off the boards. This was not as easy as it sounds because the messengers of the gods (all of whom were called Bill Stickers) never bothered to remove the old pictures but pasted new ones on top, piece by piece, until the paper was as tough and thick as leather. The great pictures were often left with strips hanging from them, fluttering in the wind and, on wet and windy days, the hoardings looked like the paper strips that rattled on the electric fan in the chip shop. I admit I tested the thickness of a curling corner once but I knew deep down that Tom or Austin was watching and I chickened out. I thought of the size of the letters they would use to write my name in the book of retribution.

It was some years later before I began to see the tattered posters as eyesores and was pleased to find them disappearing from our townscapes. But nature abhors a vacuum and the graffiti boys took over any surface they could find that could be written upon – 'Open the second front NOW' was the first salvo I remember but since then 'Kilroy was here' has developed to such an extent that Mount Olympus will never be the same again. Can you imagine the tatty, anonymous crew up there now with their grubby fingers on their pressurised paint cans, sniffing glue and waiting for inspiration? Come back the Bisto kids – all is forgiven.

It was in our school that one of the great art movements started. Most of them are fairly gradual but ours was instantaneous. It was a moment I will never forget. There was, one morning, a strange unrest throughout the building: a muted murmuring of voices and shuffling of feet which quickly grew into a stampede for the door. I was sucked into the vortex and carried along in the throng. We launched ourselves into the school yard like hungry penguins going back to sea and were joined in the asphalt ocean by streams of kids from the 'big school'. Everyone was looking up, some were pointing with trembling fingers and a few were crying – and no wonder. There over our heads and, as far as we were concerned, near enough to touch with a long pole, was the most awesome sight we had ever seen. It was an enormous glittering silver sausage with ribs, bigger than our street, and it hung there in the dusty blue sky, drifting slowly and silently over the chimney pots with 'R 101' in big black letters painted on its side. I knew then exactly how the shepherds, abiding in the fields, felt when the choirs of angels came down from heaven. And thenceforth the free balloons from Blackler's lost their glamour.

Unfortunately the silver sausage ruined imaginative chalk drawing for the rest of my time in the infants' school. Every kid in the school would have given up a week of playtimes to have got their hands on a piece of silver chalk. The classroom, from then on, was festooned with pictures of white sausages above red rooftops. Why they were always red I cannot imagine as the entire town was roofed with grey slate but I think perhaps we had stumbled into symbolism. The whole incident was a great leveller of artistic endeavour. Everyone could draw a white sausage so everyone did. We had a similar problem after the war with action painting – after all, everyone can throw paint. I myself made an attempt to break out of the side-on sausage formula but anyone who has ever tried to draw a sausage end-on will understand the difficulty. The teacher – to her credit – pinned my drawing up with the rest but called it 'Harvest Moon'. Even an infant knows there's no answer to *that*.

Me with Alan (above),
with our mother (above right)
and with our father (right)
in the yard at Crofton Road.

Soon after this we moved into the big school and into the Dark Ages. There the only teaching aid I remember being regularly employed was a big thick cane in a cupboard in the assembly hall. (The teachers always sent the unfortunate victim to fetch it while the rest of the class waited like a crowd at a public hanging.) There were ugly rumours of exams and scholarships: art went underground. There were some lighter moments, of course, and I noticed early in life that even when situations became really difficult a single word or gesture delivered at exactly the right moment could turn fear to hilarity or dispel tension faster than any wonder-drug.

There was Ronnie Thomas's hair, for example. All the boys in our class had untidy fringes of the kind often seen nowadays on middle-aged swingers who want to look 'with it'. All, that is, except Ronnie Thomas whose hair was neatly parted and thrown back in glistening black waves. One day Miss Oxford was giving the boys a roasting while the girls smirked and giggled at us. She delivered a withering verbal attack on our tatty hairstyles and said that she wanted to see an immediate change in our slipshod attitude to such things.

'Look at Ronnie Thomas,' she said. 'His hair's a credit to the school. If he can do it, so can the rest of you. What do you put on *your* hair, Ronnie?'

'Lard, Miss.' Miss Oxford's face contorted as if she'd just stepped onto the live rail of the Mersey Railway.

'Get out! Get out of this classroom immediately, you disgusting boy, and don't let me catch you . . .' etc.

Another moment of delight comes to mind.

'Violet, what are people called who live in Arabia?'

'Arabs, Miss.'

'Very good! Kenneth, what are people called who live in Germany?'

'Germans, Miss.'

'Correct. Jack Copple! Pay attention when I'm talking! What would you call people who live in Turkey?'

'Turkeys, Miss.'

Shrieks of uncontrolled hilarity. Hoots and howls and some kids literally rolling in the aisles. Oh yes, there were *some* lighter moments. The general attitude of the children however was encapsulated in the jingle which we often sang:

Mr Mumby's a very good man.
He goes to church on Sundays
And prays to God to give him strength
To cane the kids on Mondays.

It puzzled me why the little girls at school seemed to be so much wiser than us boys. They tended to gather in small groups and whisper to each other whilst keeping a weather-eye open to make sure no boys could overhear them. It was a strange sort of adult activity which so fired my curiosity that one day I gate-crashed a trio of them when they were standing in an empty classroom examining a piece of folded paper.

'What's that?' I demanded.

'Promise not to knock it out of my hand and I'll show you,' said Betty Slater. At eight years old she seemed to know all the secrets of the universe, including what little boys are likely to do to a piece of folded paper that little girls are examining.

'OK,' I said. 'Cross my heart and spit in my hat.'

She opened the folded paper which contained some white powder.

'What is it?' I asked.

'Powder,' said Betty.

'What's it for?' I said and she whipped the paper away before I could bang it underneath. The three girls looked at me pityingly and rolled their eyes.

'To put on your face, of course, stupid,' they said. 'Look, we'll show you.'

And they did. I fought back a bit at first but you can't hit girls and anyway the powder smelt quite nice – and come to that, so did they. They'd used the whole packet when Mr Cross the janitor put his head through the doorway and shouted, 'Clear out of there you lot or I'll lock you in,' and we scattered.

I noticed my mother looking a bit curiously at me across the tea-table.

'Are you feeling all right, Norm?' she said. 'You look as white as a sheet. Do you feel sick?'

'No,' I said. 'I'm OK.'

'You're *not* OK,' she said, getting up from her chair and looking very concerned. 'I think we'd better get you to bed.' She came over and peered closely at me. 'You've got face-powder on. I can smell it,' she said. 'What on earth are you doing with face-powder on?'

There was no way out so I told them what Betty and her henchwomen had done. It was mortifying. I had to go and wash my face while everyone was shrieking with laughter.

Meanwhile, in the outside world I had an irresistible compulsion to draw almost everything I saw. The reason for this, I think, was that every problem we were faced with at school after the first year or two seemed to be another trap laid by grown-ups to catch us out, whereas drawing things was easy by comparison. The answers to what things looked like were there in front of us – like being allowed to do sums with the answer page open. One thing puzzled me, however. While most of my friends and acquaintances seemed to cope better than I did with the riddles of sums and spelling, they seemed totally unable to put down on paper the things that were there before their eyes. It was an almost universal blind spot from which even the teachers seemed to suffer.

Birkenhead was a highly industrial town but this did not prevent me from being fascinated by animals and the countryside. A penny bus-ride from the bottom of the street took us to lush meadows full of cattle and wild flowers and we walked down quiet lanes bedecked with trees and butterflies. There were Sunday school treats, too, to the lake at Raby or to Dibbensdale and, although money was scarce, we sometimes had a week's holiday at a farm in North Wales and I loved the place with all my heart.

Children love to keep pets which they catch themselves. (From *Brat Race*.)

But there were still quite a lot of animals in town. There was the milkman's pony, the saltman's big brown shire with shaggy legs and the prancing giants that pulled the brewer's drays. But most of all there were the great glistening, muscular creatures that struck sparks from the stone sets beneath the overhead railway on Liverpool's waterfront. They leaned into their collars, muscles bulging, steel-shod hooves pawing for a grip before the huge carts, piled high with bales of cotton, moved forward like sailing ships.

In our own street the rag and bone man would halt his raggle-taggle cart and blow a blast on his battered trumpet that would have lifted the hearts of the English army at Agincourt on St Crispin's Day. We watched and waited for his old horse to charge but it only blinked into its blinkers and broke wind.

Industrial town or not, I clearly remember a whole herd of cows pouring through the main streets on its way to the lairage on a number of occasions. It was a sight worth watching too in the busy shopping areas like the Old Chester Road. The drover was a scruffy character called Snowball, with a gammy leg and the reputation among the children of the area that he had never washed in his whole life. He belaboured the animals' hides with a long stick and their ears with dreadful epithets as they panicked in the traffic and ran amok in the Co-op or the Home and Colonial Stores. The women who ran screaming from the shops were in as much danger from Snowball's stick as from the bellowing cattle. Occasionally things got so out of hand that the scene resembled the bull run at Pamplona, but I do not recall anyone getting seriously hurt.

The Old Chester Road may have lacked the romance of the Chisholme Trail but there were times when the cinema manager at the Coliseum, in his dark suit, white shirt-front and dicky-bow, had to head off a stampede which threatened to overrun the foyer of his picture palace while Hopalong Cassidy was doing much the same thing on the screen inside with the aid of a pair of six-shooters.

Those days were near enough to the First World War for Armistice Day to be observed with great solemnity each year. At exactly eleven o'clock in the morning on 11 November motor horns and ships' hooters would blare and everything and everybody would stand quite still in the streets wherever they were and whatever they were doing; and complete silence would descend upon the world for two minutes in memory of the dead. Children in push-chairs were hushed by their mothers, older ones warned not to move a muscle and many adults stood stiffly to attention, some with their eyes closed. I was just outside Danny Blackfern's open-fronted fish and greengrocery shop one year when the whole population froze on the spot.

There was a little brown mongrel dog sniffing round the wicker baskets of fruit and vegetables near the door of the shop and the silence was so intense that I could hear its every snuffle, and so could Danny who was standing stiffly at attention near the fish slab. His eyes, however, were following every movement of the little dog as if they were on stalks. The animal didn't seem to be aware of the silence for a moment or two but suddenly he raised his head and looked around at the unmoving human tableau. He was obviously astonished. He tried a few more probing sniffs – still no human reaction. That animal came as near to smiling as a dog can and trotted straight past Danny, through the shop and into the storeroom at the back where supplies of rabbits and poultry were kept. Danny was grinding his teeth and his face went puce but he dared not move a muscle for two agonising minutes while the mongrel sorted noisily through the stockroom. When the hooters blared again Danny reached the back room in a few giant strides and I could hear crates and boxes flying everywhere. A moment later the mongrel streaked back through the shop like a whippet, with a mouthful of feathers.

There were plenty of dogs and cats about where we lived and few people bothered, or could afford, to have their pets neutered, with the result that they (the dogs and cats) tended to make public exhibitions of themselves. We kids, unlike many country-bred children, had no idea what they were up to, but there was always some wag about who told us that the one in front was blind and the one behind was pushing it to St Dunstan's. It puzzled me why, if that were so, angry housewives would sometimes hurl buckets of water at the poor creatures from their front doors and threaten to give us the same treatment if we didn't clear off. Animals in the country always seemed to take life more placidly than those in the town. They stood

There were plenty of dogs and cats about.
(From *Magnificat*.)

about in summer fields chewing the cud, leaned their heads over rickety gates waiting for hikers to pat their noses or curled up against sun-warm cottage walls and dozed the gentle afternoons away. Their urban counterparts, on the other hand, were caught up in the human rat race and tore about in a frenzy from morning until night. I remember two dogs chasing each other down Oriel Road at about 60 m.p.h. The leading animal streaked straight across the main road at the bottom without encountering any obstacle but his pursuer reached the thoroughfare at exactly the same moment as an Austin Seven, driven sedately by a man in a bowler hat. The dog's head struck the driver's door with the sound of a Salvation Army bass drum. It fell on its back and spun round like a dazed bluebottle as the little car screeched to a halt. Women shoppers screamed and shopkeepers ran to their doors. The dog got up, blinked and took off after its playmate before the bowler hat could get out of his car. The entire door panel below the glass was stove in.

I soon found myself able to make fairly reasonable drawings of animals in the country but the townies were a different matter – they always moved too fast for close study. The fast movers were a joy to watch, however. I have always found something endearing about any living creature in full flight from some real or imaginary danger and I still find it difficult to paint a cow in a field which doesn't look as if it is ready to get the hell out of it at any moment.

The child's world is often full of mysteries and children suffer a great deal of confusion due to the slack pronunciation of most adults. I think this is true whatever part of the country one happens to be born in. I was rather thrown by the desire of adults in Sunday school and church to have God change his name to 'Arrowhead'. Well, what other reason could they have had for chanting 'Our Father which art in heaven, Arrowhead be thy name . . .'? We are all guilty, I suppose; for when David, our own son, returned home from his first day at school he asked us why they sang about Martin (the little boy who sat next to him) having to walk. We asked what he meant. 'Well', he said, 'the teacher taught us to sing "Onward Christian soldiers, Martin has to walk".'

Things could be very confusing when I was a child. Parents in our community tended to send their children to the shops to 'do the messages' which was the colloquialism for 'errands'. Sometimes we forgot or became a bit confused with the instructions given to us. On one occasion I was quite frightened by the roars of laughter from the crowded bakery shop at the bottom of our street when I pushed my mother's shopping basket up onto the counter and asked for two fresh old maids. The story spread quickly up the street until my mother heard about it and even she laughed as loudly as the rest. It seemed that the bread she liked best was called 'home-made' and it was two of those she had sent me to purchase.

Although the late twenties and most of the thirties were years of hardship and unemployment in the industrial towns of the north country, life was interesting and exciting for us children. My father worked for fifty years in various parts of Lever Bros factory at Port Sunlight. He did maintenance work on machinery but never told us much about it. Perhaps our family was luckier than many others because my father was never out of work and it is difficult to feel deprived as a child when one is warm and well fed and when one's parents are caring and responsible. It was a fact, however, that money was scarce for almost everyone and we quickly learned that when we were told that we could not have something we wanted that was the end of that and it was no use pleading.

One of the great advantages of the time was the fact that traffic compared to the present day was very thin on the ground and the streets were safe to play in. We were far more likely to be knocked down by another kid on roller skates or have our shins barked by an orange box on pram wheels with two or three children on board, than to come into contact with a bus or car, provided of course that we didn't play in the centre of a main road. Even the fact that economic conditions of the time made life extremely difficult for many adults turned out to provide us children with fun and excitement.

Traffic dangers were caused mainly by other children.
(From *Top Dog.*)

In an effort to eke out a livelihood many individuals and small groups of men travelled about the towns putting on impromptu performances in the street and going round with a hat. It was lovely. We used to sit along the edge of the kerb and watch men in slightly soiled but still magnificent highland dress doing the sword dance outside our own front doors. Groups of ex-servicemen with medals jingling on their patched clothes would play on cornets or piano accordions while another would do a clog dance in the centre of the street. One-man-bands were a common diversion, and we would stand around them so close that we were in danger of getting our heads trapped between their cymbals as we tried to work out how one man could play so many instruments at one time and produce such a marvellous ear-splitting din.

One regular visitor to our street was the barrel-organ man. He was a bit sinister in appearance, very tall and dressed in an old mackintosh which fell away from his shoulders like a bell tent that had had its guy ropes cut. He wore a high-crowned trilby hat and his chin was the colour of a livid bruise. I never heard him utter a word to anyone and wondered whether it was due to the fact that the yellow 'dog-end' which was always between his thin lips had sealed them forever. All the same, I envied and admired him. It was not so much the beautiful jangling tunes which he could produce from the grubby canvas-covered organ, it was the way he could turn the handle with one hand as he stared up the road and then, when the mood took him, change to the other hand and stare down the road without the slightest hiccup in the rhythmic music. As far as I was concerned it was the acme of musical skill and once or twice I saw someone give him something for doing it.

There were few entertainments of this kind however that could match the fascination of the escapologists. They came in pairs carrying a big canvas bag and a mass of jingling chains with padlocks attached. They would set up their pitch against the gable-end of a house in our street and one would deliver a lively speech about the world-wide fame of the other scruffy Herbert who was standing by, keeping a sharp eye open both up and down the street. When a small crowd had gathered – a crowd which seemed to consist entirely of children who had nothing more valuable than a few conkers and a bit of string in their pockets (how did these men ever earn a crust?), the speaker would handcuff his partner and drape him with chains and padlocks before helping him inside the sack. He would then padlock the top of the sack and wind yards of chain round and round his mate and fix the lot firmly with several more locks. The escapologist would then fall down on the pavement and writhe about like a clubbed rabbit whilst the other took over the task of watching both ends of the street. Mostly the captive would emerge like magic from his sack after a decent display of agonised struggling and the crowd would melt away as quickly as it had gathered. On one occasion, however, the escape merchant had hardly hit the pavement when his partner stepped across and kicked the sack just about where his mate's ribs would be and he shot out of the sack like a ferret, gathered up the sack and chains and the pair of them disappeared up Moorland Road before we knew what was happening. They were out of sight by the time I noticed the policeman walking up the street.

Sunday mornings were punctuated by marching bands. There was the Boys' Brigade and the Boy Scouts (known always as the Sky Bouts). You could hear them coming for miles, the steady thump, thump, thump of the drums and the sudden staccato blast of massed bugles all hitting slightly different notes. It was lovely. A bit later in the day the Salvation Army would strike up. Their music was of a distinctly higher quality; even the children in uniform who marched behind never hit the bitter-sweet discords the Baden-Powell kids could manage. The Sally Bonks could put on a good show and in some parts of the town the local people would bring chairs out from their houses and sit around in the street joining in the singing of 'Rock of Ages Cleft for Me' or 'The Old

We played lots of street games.
(From *Brat Race*.)

And we loved blood-curdling ghost stories.
(From *Brat Race*.)

Wooden Cross' until the tears streamed down their faces.

Every day of the week had its own distinct character and feel, difficult to describe but nonetheless real for that. Indeed, I saw each day as having its own colour, as clear and vivid as the stained glass in the lobby door. The year, too, was divided into distinct sections according to the street games we played. In the dark winter evenings the gas-lamppost was the 'den' and we played a variety of hide-and-seek games behind the privet hedges of the tiny front gardens of neighbours' houses. The one who was 'it' would creep out from the den and anyone he caught hiding was taken back to the den and was honour-bound to stay there until all players were roped in, unless someone could creep out from their hiding place and get to the lamppost before 'it', slap the metal and shout 'Relievio'. All prisoners could then scatter into the darkness once more and 'it' had to start all over again.

When the weather got cold we made winter warmers from clay that we dug up with old spoons in the daisy field. The clay was fashioned into small rectangular or round containers with holes in the sides. We put bits of rag into them and held a match to them until the rag began to smoulder, then ran like mad round the streets to get enough through-draught to keep them burning. Half an hour of that and even those whose burners had gone out or disintegrated were so hot that they had to take off their scarves and gloves and fan themselves with their caps.

We loved telling each other blood-curdling ghost stories and sometimes we would put a candle in a jamjar and advance up a dark back-entry in a tight, terrified knot chanting, 'Oompah, Oompah, stick it up your jumpar', and then, struck by sudden panic and terror, we would race back down the entry to the warm security of the gaslit street. We lost a number of candles and jamjars doing that.

Another winter game was to tie a reel of black cotton onto someone's front door knocker and carry the thread across the road to a suitable hiding place. By jerking the cotton we could give a really good hammering to the door and when the owners came out and peered up and down the dark street it was difficult not to giggle. This technique could be carried to exquisite lengths by giving the door another smart rap as soon as the irate householders had closed it. When they came steaming out again shouting for vengeance our nerve usually cracked and we would scatter into the darkness, deliciously frightened. There was hoop time and conkers time and marbles time and whip-and-top and hop-scotch time and yo-yo time and biff-bat time – and we followed them all with the unquestioning devotion of the primitive sub-species to which all the world's children belong.

In summer we played nameless team games of our own invention: like grabbing a cap from the centre of the road and trying to reach the opposite pavement without being touched by the one who was 'it', whose job it was to touch us before we were 'home' with the cap. If he touched us we were 'it' and he could join the team on the pavement and have a go himself. Then there was 'Weak Horse' which the girls never joined in. We split into two teams and the team leader would bend forward and lean against a wall and his team would do the same behind him to form a line. The other team would line up behind each other on the opposite pavement and their leader would run as fast as possible and leap as far along the line of bent backs as he could. The rest would follow, one at a time, until all were on the backs of the horses. If the line of horses gave way under the strain they had to be horses again but if they held up for a count of ten the teams changed over.

We went to the local parks and played football with an old tennis ball and cricket with the same ball, and heaved each other up to get a drink from the cast-iron fountain set among laurel bushes. Those who were too small to reach the trickling water across the fountain bowl would use a laurel

We spent a lot of time playing in the shrubberies at Victoria and Mersey parks. (From *Brat Race*.)

leaf to bridge the gap between their mouths and the water. Sometimes we went to the daisy field and made a tent with two sticks and a discarded bed sheet, which was owned by Charlie East. Charlie had sisters a lot older than himself and picked up smatterings of their grown-up conversation so that he seemed always to have some gems of knowledge to impart to us. Gandhi was going to start a war, he told us; Mussolini had a secret death-ray with which he could kill everybody in the world without getting out of bed; the church organist had made off with the poor-box and the lady from the wool shop.

One day he came down the street to join our gang, bobbing and weaving and ducking his head like a featherweight boxer. Even when we were playing dribbling-shots-in against old Ma Parsons's gable end he was still at it, feinting this way and that and parrying invisible adversaries. You live longer if you do it, he told us. Why? Because germs blow about in the air and if one gets in your mouth or up your nose you'd be a gonner. If you dodge about it's more difficult for them to find the hole so they bounce harmlessly off your head. Charlie was wrong about the poor-box but not about the lady from the wool shop.

Shops in general were fascinating places in those days. Every single one had its own character and smell which was quite different from any other. Martin Eddy had a fish shop just three doors up the street from us where the walls were hand-painted with magnificent seascapes which showed trawlers and drifters tossing about in mountainous seas. On the white frieze above the paintings were preserved specimens of exotic fish; a sunfish like a football with sharp spines all over, the sword from a swordfish, a flying fish and a dragonfish from the South Seas. On a shelf behind his counter was a sailing ship in a bottle, and a wooden cross in another which Martin said was cut from the cross on which Christ was crucified.

It was a haven of startling smells and exotic marvels and Martin didn't seem to mind how much I hung about his shop and followed him around. Indeed, he must have loved children, although he had none of his own, for he used to take me with him on his Saturday morning fish round. He had a motor bike combination and had replaced the side-car with a large fish box which had its own chopping block and scales. There was a metal grill pillion seat behind Martin's own seat, which had no cushion and could be quite vicious on my anatomy as we bounced along in a cloud of blue smoke but I loved going with him and listening to his repertoire of pleasantries exchanged with the housewives who came out to buy a filleted

Every shop had its own particular character.
This cartoon was published in Punch *in 1952 and* Thelwell Country.

plaice or a 'nice piece of cod'. His favourite parting shot was, 'With my looks and your money, my dear, we could make sweet music together.' I'm sure everyone of them had heard it many times before but they always smiled and said, 'Get away with you, Martin.' They knew, as I did, that he was a gentle man.

Miss Jones kept the milk shop next door where we were sent with an enamel jug (so that you wouldn't cut yourself when you fall over) to collect a gill of milk. She was unimaginably old and her speech had been replaced by grunts. She had a little roly-poly curly-coated terrier with vicious eyes, yellow teeth and the instincts of a piranha fish. Neither of them liked children. Her shop was completely bare except for a milk churn in the middle of the floor.

The two brothers who kept the greengrocery shop on the corner were huge men, completely dominated by their mother who always wore black button-up boots and a black cape which covered everything down to her ankles. They weren't all that fond of kids but, to be fair, they had good reason. As the boxes and wicker baskets became empty they would stack them up outside the window to keep the shop floor clear and at fairly regular intervals one kid or another would run up the street, kick the bottom basket away and be at a safe distance before the brothers could lay hands on them. They were collecting up their baskets one day when Mrs Cook from number thirty-four told them in no uncertain terms that it was disgusting to call words like that after little children.

It was about this time that I had my first encounter with a horse; one that wasn't pulling something at the time, that is, and wasn't safely fenced in a field. Most people got only one week's holiday per year from their work and were not always too certain of that, so it was great to be spending seven days on a farm in North Wales. I loved the place with all my heart and in retrospect I still do. The farmer had two shire horses and was taking them to be shod at the forge about half a mile away. He asked Alan and me whether we

would like to go along and when we said yes he heaved my brother up on one giant animal and me onto the other and told us to hang on tight. He then planted his ample boot into the fleshy rump of each animal and shouted something in Welsh. They set off at a fast clip down the steep, narrow lanes with Alan and me bouncing this way and that and hanging on to their flying manes for dear life. We were delivered to the forge about ten minutes before the farmer ambled up.

Everything about that little farm near Corwen was idyllic as far as I was concerned and we spent many holidays there after the first visit. It impressed itself so deeply on my mind that I could still draw the place from almost every angle to this day and probably get the right number of panes in each window and the right trees in the right places – at least as they were in the thirties. We learned how to milk the cows, feed and lead the horses and drive the horse-drawn reapers and rakes (I don't think there were many laws about safety for children or workers on farms in those days) and, after working in the hayfields all day, it was lovely to ride back to the stackyard on top of the high swaying loads. I remember with delight climbing tired into the deep feather bed in a room with polished wooden floorboards and silky white sheepskins scattered by the bedside. Just before sleep one could hear the leaves rustling on the trees outside and the enchanting noises of the approaching summer night. On Wednesday nights I felt a tight pain in my stomach as I lay in bed, for it was the apex of the week which would now slope downwards to Saturday morning when we would walk down the lanes with our cases to the tiny station at Derwen and sit watching the cattle grazing as we waited and watched for the smudge of distant smoke that heralded the approach of the steam engine which would take us back to town.

(above) Llys Farm in North Wales where we spent summer holidays. It was painted in 1980 from a colour sketch done in 1940 and a tiny, dim photograph but mainly from memory.
(below) Colour sketch of stream in the Clwyd Valley.

Me on the horse rake

*and on the hay cart with
the farmer's daughters and my mother.*

Sadness and regret does not last long for children, however, because the whole world is full of magic. Our own Cheshire countryside was but a stone's throw away when we were at home and the River Mersey, although huge and turgid compared to the Clwyd, was the very centre of the shipping world where every great liner ever built could be seen at one time or another, swinging at anchor or against the stages of the Liverpool waterfront. It was a very different magic to that of the hilly Welsh farms but no less intense to stand on Rock Ferry pier and watch the ferries coming and going and see the paddle-steamer plying upstream to Eastham. Even set against the great liners, the Mersey ferries were attractively strong, chunky boats and on the floating landing-stage at Woodside the atmosphere was intense and exciting. I can still hear the rattle of chains and the crash of gangways, the clang-clang of the brass bell and the smell of ropes and tar.

In those days Nelson's navy was still represented there by the wooden warship *Conway* anchored permanently in the river as a naval training ship. It was the black-and-white pattern of the gunports which impinged upon my mind as I fell from my first bicycle and was catapulted over the edge of the esplanade, head first onto the rocks about ten or twelve feet below. I was lucky to survive that awful moment and still have scars across my eye lids and cheek to remember it by.

Self-portrait. This is the earliest drawing which still survives. I was ten at the time and my mother had allowed me to stay away from school because I was not feeling well. I must have made a quick recovery because I made the drawing sitting up in bed with a mirror propped up against my knees. I cannot remember who added the inscription, top left, but it is in red ink so I think it must have been added by a school teacher.

Barnston Cottages, c. 1937:
one of my earliest attempts
at landscape paintings.

2: TRAINING FOR LIFE

About this time we moved from the warm exciting street to the slightly more sedate suburbs where everyone was semi-detached and bluetits condescended to mingle from time to time with the house sparrows in the handkerchief-sized gardens. I moved on from the non-art primary school to a non-art grammar school which was housed in two large Victorian residences called Ravenswood House and Stoneleigh about three hundred yards apart and all surrounded by playing fields and a modest stretch of woodland. There were rugby and cricket pitches but the only hints of an educational nature to be found within Stoneleigh were the blackboards screwed to the bedroom walls, the random scattering of desks and chairs and the fact that the carved wood and marble fireplaces were filled with old gym shoes and the dusty caps of whichever pupils were being bullied at the time.

The large rooms at Ravenswood House were equipped as physics and chemistry labs, but the rest of the form rooms were as domestic as those at Stoneleigh. We were given to understand that the school had traditions which must be observed at all costs but the only ones I came across in five years were that we were obliged to play rugby, which most of us hated, and forbidden to play football, which we liked; and that it was a heinous offence to walk across a cricket pitch with braces on. I do not recollect being given a single word of instruction on any games.

It was stony ground for the visual arts. We had a double period of art once a week in a double-sized bedroom where we were given precise instructions as to what we were to draw. Subjects ranged from a matchbox with the tray slightly open to a ladder propped against a wall. During end of term or annual exams we were likely to be asked to draw a corkscrew leaning against a bottle or a tin opener on a fruit can, just to take the steam out of anyone who was getting too big for his boots. In one lesson the subject was a dog kennel. A double period was a long time to sit without talking or moving out of our chairs and I defy anyone to take more than a few minutes to draw a dog kennel. To relieve the bordom I put a dog half in and half out of the kennel and was just working out whether his floppy ears would touch the ground when his head was stretched out along his paws when a shadow loomed over me.

'What are you supposed to be doing?'

'Drawing, sir.'

'*What* are you drawing?'

'A dog, sir.'

'Who told you to draw a dog?'

'No one, sir.'

The art master detached my paper from the drawing-board without removing the drawing pins and handed me a clean sheet of paper.

'What did I tell you to draw?'

'A dog kennel, sir.'

'Right! Get on with it lad. I'll tell you when I want you to draw a dog.'

But he never did.

NORMAN THELWELL.
1939

28

I won the art prize once – went up onto the stage at the town hall on speech day, applauded by parents and hated by my peers, like all rotten swots. I was given a limp handshake – 'Well done lad!' – and a book on drawing which had the school crest embossed in gold on the back. It contained line drawings of matchboxes with the trays slightly open, ladders propped against walls and, among the advanced studies near the end, a corkscrew leaning against a bottle and a can opener on a tin of fruit. Artists, I have noticed, love to tell how they spent the bulk of their time at school drawing in the margins of their exercise books. They wouldn't have done it twice at our school. I tried it once and spent the next Wednesday afternoon in detention writing a piece on the evils of wasting paper.

(left) I made so many drawings of my cat in 1939–40 that he would lie or sit up for quite long periods with no more movement than gentle swaying when he began to doze off.

(below) I tended to add dramatic titles to my cat drawings, such as 'The Hunter Hunted' or 'A Narrow Escape', but he refused to pose for action shots.

JAN·18·1940.   'THE SILENT RAIDER'.   NORMAN THELWELL.

My grammar-school education consisted almost entirely of being told what to read in which books in the evening at home and being tested on it the next day in the form rooms. As an educational establishment it had one great advantage over our primary school in that the cane, or 'the stick' as it was known, was reserved for serious misdemeanours and (as far as I know) was administered in the secrecy of the headmaster's study – or Gaffer's Boudoir – for I was never caned again and suffered no more physical violence than the odd cuff across the head. I applauded this great step forward but could never quite work out the logic of it. Presumably adults felt that once a boy had reached eleven years of age his mind and body could no longer stand the trauma of having his fingers beaten blue with a cane for spelling a few words wrongly or whispering during morning assembly. If that was the case then one was bound to assume that the ladies who taught us up to the eleven-plus (or scholarship) thought that such treatment was beneficial to children during the first ten years of life.

It is only fair to point out that we were not caned in the infants' classes. A sharp crack across the knuckles with a ruler was all we ever suffered there; although I do remember several boys of tender years being hauled out and put across a certain pedagogue's knee in front of the class. She would then haul on the leg of his short pants to expose as much of his little bum as possible and clout it with her open hand. I don't think it did much damage there, though it made an alarming noise, but she would stretch the pants so tightly that heaven knows what she was doing to other important little places. I don't remember any little girls being caned in the junior school, but my wife tells me that at the village school which she attended at that age the girls were given the same 'spare the rod and spoil the child' treatment as the boys, so perhaps I was taught by forward thinkers after all.

Our grammar-school gymnasium was located in what must have been the coach house in former days and it was presided over by a very likeable gentleman who was so overweight that he spent most of his time sitting the wrong way round on a chair and leaning on the chairback. The gym was also used for singing lessons and in order to protect the wood-block floor we had to remove our shoes before going in. Once inside we were required to stand in lines on the heavy wooden gymnasium forms, but whether this was to protect the floor or our socks I am not sure. It may have been to enable the singing master to put his ear closer to our faces without bending down too far when he was selecting young blood for the Operatic Society or Speech Day choir. I have no reason to suppose that the personal hygiene of my classmates was below average but thirty little boys in their stockinged feet gave off an atmosphere which was memorable, to say the least; and I cannot hear those beautiful lines,

> On wings of song I bear thee to those far
>   Asian lands,
> Where the broad wave of the Ganges flows
>   down through those flower-strewn lands,

without sixty hot socks coming to my mind. It's much the same with 'Come into the garden Maud'.

We attended school on Saturday mornings and had Wednesday afternoons off to compensate unless we happened to collect a Wednesday detention. I liked the arrangement because of the free afternoon and Saturday mornings had something of the end of term feeling, too. Even the masters seemed to feel the same way, for the eternal tests were often shelved until the next Monday; and Joe Egg, the English master, would take a book of verse or essays, sit himself comfortably on a desk with his feet on a chair and read to us in his beautifully modulated voice. To me those were the few golden hours of school, as his words poured over us like the sunshine that slanted through the high, dusty windows, and they opened up a magic world of pleasure and delight.

He was called 'Joe Egg' because on Merseyside

everyone's name was either shortened, changed to something which sounded vaguely similar (e.g. a boy named Towers was known as Towser) or they were given a quite different name with the same initials. Thus, Joseph Evans would become 'Joe Egg' and Richard Smith would be known as 'Dick Spit' – quite simple really!

The only text book we were required to have for art lessons was a slim volume on English church architecture. It was a simple book dealing with the main styles from Saxon through Norman, Early English, Decorated and Perpendicular but, like Joe Egg's reading sessions, to me it was the key to a new and life-long interest.

I decided to draw all the old parish churches in the Wirral and write a best-seller about the whole shebang. From then on I spent almost all my free time touring the peninsula on my bike and drawing the old parish churches and other buildings which I considered to be of architectural interest. It was a

My pen-and-ink drawings of churches and other buildings were done on the spot, but I was influenced by the work of other artists and was inclined to add sky effects and a frame when I got them home.

APRIL. 27. m. 1940.

NORMAN THELWELL.

WOODCHURCH.

most absorbing pastime and took my mind off the worries of looming exams and the need to find a job when they were over. Even the war-clouds, which had been gathering since my infancy, could be forgotten for a few hours.

Having completed a number of drawings, I decided to handle the literary side of my project at the same time and opened chapter one with a description of my first trip to Woodchurch. I began with the weather, the drawing materials I took with me and what was in the sandwiches my mother put in my saddlebag. It was at that point that the narrative began to drag a bit and I decided to postpone serious literature until I had more artwork ready. By the time Neville Chamberlain got back from Munich with his little sheet of paper I had about twenty drawings finished. My Uncle Jim said he thought they were very good and asked me if he could borrow them to show to a friend.

He returned a week later with four or five of them and announced that he had sold the rest to his friend for half-a-crown. The few returns, he told me, were those his pal felt were not quite up to scratch. Even in those days 2*s.* 6*d.* barely covered the cost of nibs, ink and paper used, to say nothing of wear and tear on my bicycle and about sixty hours' work. At 2*d.* per drawing there didn't seem much future in art as a profession.

At a time when Britain was so lamentably short of arms to defend itself against the Nazis there was one boy in our form at school who was trying to do something about it. Like Betty Slater in the primary school, he tended to carry powder about in his pockets, contained in small boxes and screws of paper. It wasn't face-powder, however, but gunpowder which he made himself at home and, being in a more or less experimental stage, it was a bit unreliable. We gathered round him in tight,

A lady who was cleaning the church while I was working asked me if I would give her the drawing.
I managed to hang on to it by telling her that I needed it for a book I was writing
and I felt guilty for weeks after for telling a white lie in church.

THE THAW. MARSH LANE. WIRRAL.

We were given a half-day holiday from the office on New Year's Day, 1940. It was bitterly cold and I forgot to take my sketching stool when I went out sketching in the afternoon. The owner of the farm on the left kindly lent me a milking stool. Again, the sky, frame and signature were added at home to give it a 'professional' look.

curious groups at break-time in secret corners of the school woods to watch him testing his latest mixture. Sometimes it produced a bit of smoke and flame and an awful stink but from time to time he blew a tin can several feet into the air. He was known as 'the Professor' and we admired him greatly. He used to invite a few of us into his house on the way home from school to watch him continue his research indoors. We never once saw his parents who, presumably, both went out to work. He was deliciously irresponsible and on one occasion he burned a hole in the carpet and we had to open the windows to get rid of the acrid smoke. His mother was so upset that she forbade any further explosions inside her house. It was only

a temporary setback however for, as he explained, if we all moved the piano away from the wall he could work there and any damage to the floor would be hidden when the piano was pushed back into place. All might have been well if he had not put a syrup tin over his new, improved powder before igniting it. The tin flew straight up in the air and knocked a big lump of plaster out of the ceiling. We cleaned up the mess and put the piano back all neat and tidy but it was the end as far as the rest of us were concerned. The Professor went over to making miniature cannons on his father's lathe in the cellar and we were forbidden to go to the house. I often wondered a few years later how they went on in the blitz.

By this time we were beginning to get girl-conscious. We knew all about face-powder and things like that but all the grammar schools were strictly segregated and we boys tended to gather in bunches on our bicycles at strategic crossroads where many of the girls from Wirral County High School also congregated on their way home. It was at one of these social gatherings that Ken Williams and I started 'going with' Jean and Pamela. 'Going with' girls meant talking to them rather more than one talked to the others in the group and, with a bit of luck, meeting them on Saturday afternoon at Raby Mere or Arrow Park. One winter afternoon Jean told us that her parents would be out at choir practice that evening and that Pam would be keeping her company while they were away. If we cared to call round, she said, we would be welcome.

It was an evening of wild romance and thrilling danger. We had a game of snap, smoked a couple of Woodbines and exchanged a few tense kisses. We spoke in whispers in case we might fail to hear a footstep on the gravel path outside. A sudden knock on the front door brought all four of us to our feet, white-faced with terror.

When Jean could speak she said, 'I expect it's Daddy,' which didn't help to calm us.

The front door was adjacent to the bay window of the room we were in.

'I'll open the side window to see who it is,' whispered Jean. 'If it's Daddy I'll leave the window open and you two get ready to jump out as soon as I go round and let him in.'

It was Daddy all right and Ken and I stood by the curtained window as tense as coiled springs ready to leap for freedom when the vengeful parent walked into the hall. As soon as we heard Jean greet her father we launched ourselves out of the window like paras leaping from a plane. Unfortunately Daddy hesitated for a second before stepping inside and we both caught him at about shoulder height. He went down like a pole-axed steer and we fled into the night.

Raby Mere was one of our favourite haunts on Saturday afternoons.
(Drawing from *A Plank Bridge by a Pool*.)

3: BIG BOOTS AND BAYONETS

Taking it Easy.

Norman
Thelwell.

A pencil sketch made on board the troop-ship Silesia *bound for India.*

In 1939 things began to happen rather suddenly. I left school at the age of sixteen and the war began. It was very strange to look up into the calm, blue infinity of a Sunday morning sky and watch two or three tiny silver biplanes circling each other in a mock dog-fight like something out of *Biggles*. There was a strange tense excitement everywhere, talk of war effort, evacuees, bombing raids, gas attacks and shelters. Yet nothing changed except for silly little cardboard gas mask boxes hung on a string round everybody's shoulder and strips of sticky paper on windows here and there. We still had to get jobs and our education equipped us for nothing but life in an office. We queued, along with a string of boys from our own form at school as well as others, outside any office that advertised a vacancy. It was all about as interesting as applying to a prison for a vacant cell. Eventually, and probably as a consequence of vast numbers of men and women joining or being called up, I got a job as a junior clerk in an office quite near to the Liverpool waterfront. The work was even more dreary than at school. We worked on Saturday mornings also, as we had done at school, but there was no Wednesday afternoon off to compensate and no one read to us any more.

We had been unaware that for the last four years we had been 'teenagers' because I do not recollect that such a section of the population existed then. One was a child however long one stayed at school and expected to do whatever adults said one must. The day we left school we were men and expected to act like men, which also meant doing whatever adults said we must. Once outside the office, life could still be fun, however, for there were friends of my own age group and we were no longer segregated, so that we went about together in the evenings and at weekends and formed firm partnerships with both sexes. Although we had never been teenagers, we were acutely aware that, if we could still move and were warm to the touch, by the time we were eighteen we would be channelled into one or other of the forces. So suddenly we knew that we were into our golden years, maybe eight hundred salad days to military service with a bit of luck.. We knew we had to enjoy life while we could – and we did.

The pleasures of country walks, visits to the cinema and days spent with mixed groups of friends on Hilbre Island in the Dee estuary were heightened by the intensity of feeling and the optimism of youth and, by contrast, with the depressing news of the war and, a little later, the increasing frequency and savagery of the blitz.

My diaries for 1940 and 1941 make little reference to the office except when nights were spent on the roof firewatching with a tin hat and a stirrup pump. On the other hand, among the brief references to events like the Battle of the River Plate and the fall of France there are careful records of which landscapes or buildings I was drawing or painting at the time and accounts of being challenged by civilians, Home Guards or police and frisked for evidence that I was collecting information for despatch to Berlin. This routine was carried out with comical solemnity, even when I was drawing the dilapidated cottages near the golf links. One day, along with a friend, I was painting Neston church when a police car drew up and we were made to stand with our hands above our heads while they went through our pockets. The only item which seemed to interest them was a much-folded picture of Esther Williams in a natty swimsuit which they winkled out of my friend's wallet. They returned our identity cards and loose change, told us to remember that there was a war on and drove away with Esther Williams.

But golden days are golden days, however dark the nights, and there is a strange link in the human mind which keeps them polished and protected in nostalgic cotton wool. I find myself recalling the times with pleasure even when I read the diaries which I kept during those years:

Friday May 2nd 1941
Worked on my drawing of Walton Church this evening. We had a terrible raid tonight but Liverpool got it worse than us.

Saturday May 3rd 1941
Exchange Station was hit last night and we spent the morning helping to clear glass, dust and rubble in the office. Went to the Plaza with the gang to see *Double or Nothing*. We had another awful raid tonight. Nearly all the houses around were damaged, including ours. The All Clear came about 5.30 a.m. and it was daylight before anyone got to bed.

Sunday 4th May
Went to Eddy's farm this afternoon to draw in the stable but we spent most of the time picking up shrapnel and incendiaries in the fields.

I am surprised to find that I forgot to record that Saturday, 3 May was also my eighteenth birthday. But then I am surprised to find that I kept my diaries up-to-date at all during those terrible days.

As a group of friends we had kept together with great tenacity in spite of the bombings and general uncertainties of life. Jim lived in a fairly big house which had an old coach house in the garden and we had converted the upper floor into a club room. There was electric light and an iron stove and we had each contributed a piece of furniture until it had a warm and welcoming atmosphere. There was a half-size snooker table, too, and pictures on the wall, and I was co-opted to paint 'The Coach House Club' in large red letters on the wall above the iron stove. The boys met there with great regularity for a game of snooker or pontoon, or just to talk in the evenings; and sometimes we decorated the place, particularly just before Christmas when we had a party. Almost everything was rationed, but the girls joined forces with us and together we found enough food – and there was no rationing of party games.

Wars, I am glad to say, do not stop young men from having devastating crushes on girls and vice versa. It was one of the delights of those precious months before our group was dispersed forever. Reg was smitten suddenly by Barbara. She had been in our group for more than a year but it was as if he had never seen her before. He simply could not think of enough things to do to impress her. One very snowy Saturday afternoon, he and I had just emerged from the library on Borough Road when he spied her mincing prettily along on the other side of the road with a dainty umbrella keeping the snow off her hair. Love has the strangest effects upon young men. He handed me his books, took up a handful of snow and patted it into a firm ball and then, with the grace of a cricketer on the long on boundary he sent it flying in a perfect parabola over the pavement and busy roadway down, down with the accuracy of a three-inch mortar bomb, straight through Barbie's umbrella where it exploded into her hair-do and down her neck.

In the next few months all my friends were dispersed to various services and my own calling-up papers arrived. I don't know who Barbara eventually married but I know it wasn't Reg.

The medical which everyone went through was an experience which I would not relish going through again. It took place in a great, dismal barn of a place called Renshaw Hall in Liverpool which was swarming with people, mostly naked or nearly so. They stood about in long winding queues looking dejected and embarrassed by their own and others' nakedness and bewildered by the confusion. Men in white coats were herding and testing and prodding like prospective buyers at a cattle market. Not sure which queue to join, I stood near a long line of wood and canvas cubicles and waited to be herded, when a white-coat came along and asked what I thought I was doing.

I said I didn't know.

'Get in one of those cubby holes and get your clothes off,' it said. 'Then wait here for instructions.'

So I did. As I stood outside the cubicle with nothing on, the scene reminded me vividly of a picture I had seen in a religious book for young people which depicted, in terrifying detail, hundreds of tortured souls writhing in hell-fire. At least they had looked warm.

Another medico with a clipboard under his arm asked me what I thought I was up to standing about naked without being in a queue. I said I didn't know but that I had been told to take my clothes off and await instructions. He asked my name and ran his finger down a list on his clipboard.

'OK,' he said. 'Join that lot over there and remember next war – don't take your clothes off till I tell you.' He hurried away into the throng chortling loudly at his own wit.

As a fully paid-up card-carrying coward I had no great desire to fight anyone, but as all my friends were joining up I didn't want to be the odd one out either. So I cared little which service they thought me best suited for providing that it did not entail marching about in big boots and prodding at people with a bayonet. I had two further interviews after being declared fit to fight; one with a psychologist who read out a list of words and asked me to respond to each with the first word that came into my head, and another with a psychiatrist who showed me a lot of pieces of paper with ink blots on them and asked me what they made me think of apart from ink blots.

Shortly after this I was despatched to a one-time holiday camp at Squires Gate, near Blackpool, and provided with a pair of big boots, a First World War rifle and bayonet and a long line of dummy Germans to prod. My first impression of the Army was that it was very hairy. Our shapeless uniforms were hairy and the collars which, upon pain of serious retribution, had to be hooked up tightly under our chins, were so rough that they rubbed the skin off our chins and would have been a delight to those medieval monks who loved to mortify their flesh with hair shirts. Our shirts were of coarse material too, but less lethal. They had no collars, however: just a strip of tape round the top with a tin button so that they did not intervene between the jacket collar and our tortured skin. The shirt we wore during the day served also as our only sleeping garment over our 'vest and drawers, cellular' and was useless as a defence against the rabidly vicious hairy blankets which could skin one's nose if pulled up too high.

It was February of 1942, very cold and we were within a Mills bomb's throw of the Irish Sea. When I awoke to the first reveille there was a semi-circular sheet of rough ice on the blanket where my breath had condensed and frozen during the night. The only comfort was finding that the other boys had to crack their way out of their bunks too. I hated almost everything about the Army but I undoubtedly learned more about drawing and painting during my five or six years' service than at any other time of my life. This may have been due to the fact that I was at the right age for such development; but I'm sure that it was, in part at least, due to the endless boredom, fear and lunacy and the need to concentrate on something one could believe in beyond the present nightmare.

our kit begins to gather.

12 February 1942: the first day at the Infantry Training Centre. I had just returned from the company stores with my kit and had no idea what it was all for when I made this sketch. It is an example of the frantic way I tried to record everything I saw.

I carried my sketchbooks everywhere and drew almost literally everything whenever a moment presented itself. Reaction to my odd behaviour varied – mostly it was simple indifference. A few men asked for portraits of themselves to send home or suggested something spicy to pin on the barrack-room wall, but here and there it provoked a surprisingly bitter and violent reaction: like that of the corporal from the Welsh Guards who, during a kit inspection, rummaged in my kit bag, drew out a bundle of pencils and brushes in an elastic band and proceeded to break the whole lot in a mighty effort of strength which brought beads of sweat to his forehead. He threw the debris onto my bed and with an imperious glance around at the astonished young soldiers standing by their beds he shouted, 'How many bleeding Germans do you think you're going to kill with those?' Such was the power of one or two stripes in an infantry training centre that a few days later he summoned me to his chalet and asked me to draw a portrait of him to send home to his girlfriend in Merthyr Tydfil. Being determined to survive the war if

possible I did so and was astonished at his embarrassing gratitude. I couldn't help wondering what he had made of the psychiatrist's ink blots.

There were also those among my comrades who regarded my frenetic scribbling as eccentric and accused me of attempting to obtain my early discharge on the grounds of mental instability. As far as they were concerned it ranked with the more common method of feeding and talking to imaginary chickens on the barrack-room floor. At a time when survival was the only thing left to look forward to, the desire to record the whole manic mess became a kind of security blanket but there were times when it was of practical use also. The generally held belief that if the stripes and pips found out that you were a musician they would give you the job of moving the NAAFI piano was quite true, so that from time to time I was diverted from jumping off assault boat ramps into icy Scottish lochs and given the job of stencilling the divisional sign in three colours onto our battalion vehicles. Until I was in the forces my subject-matter for pictures had been concerned

(left) Two pen-and-ink sketches from the NAAFI canteen.

Relaxing on an army exercise.
Charcoal pencil sketch.

Washing in a Barrack Room
Hursley 42

Washing in the Nissen hut at Hursley Park Camp, Hampshire.

*Water-colour painting of a blacksmith's forge,
just outside the main gate of the army camp
where I was billeted with the East Yorkshire Regiment
in Dumfriesshire.
I made this painting one Saturday
afternoon in the summer of 1943.*

with buildings, landscape and animals and although
I had carried a small sketchbook and made
drawings of people on trains and buses, I found
figure-drawing difficult – mainly because no one
would ever keep still. Once I was in the forces
there was less time to paint landscapes or make
careful studies of buildings but humans – mostly in
uniform – surged about me everywhere and I
found a new compulsion to record turmoil and
movement.

After the infantry training centre I was posted to
Watford to join the second battalion of the East
Yorkshire Regiment. I was transferred soon after
joining to the intelligence section, where there was
a tenuous connection with drawing. We were
trained particularly for the job of setting up
observation posts in advance of the battalion
positions, from which we could (with a bit of luck)
send back information on the terrain ahead and

Having forty winks
in a road-side ditch.

possibly on enemy positions. A certain amount of skill in drawing simple landscapes, diagrams and maps was an obvious advantage and provided short breaks from the main occupation of infantry soldiers which, when there was no enemy about, was marching for mile after mile on blistered feet and digging slit trenches to spend the night in.

We obtained some relief from this boring business of marching in long columns of three (particularly when there was a fair number of civilians about) by everyone whistling a short off-key note just as their left leg came forward. It sounded as if we all had metal hip joints which needed oiling. The effect was wildly comical. The civilian population found it more entertaining than a military band. Whenever we were being loaded up into lorries, trains or ships someone would bleat loudly in the throng and in seconds everyone would take their cue so that we sounded like a vast flock of sheep on the way to the slaughterhouse. It was the only way we could make known how we felt about what was happening to us without bringing retribution down upon our heads. It is quite difficult to be sure which sheep in a herd is bleating at any particular moment.

We never spent much time in any one town or camp but moved from place to place. Whilst we were at Norris Castle next to Osborne House on the Isle of Wight we used to cross the Medina river on Saturday nights to West Cowes where there was rather more to do. The Southampton area was still under aerial attack at that time so it was all very dark as we waited on the slipway for the chain ferry to take us back to camp. A certain Sergeant Scot had imbibed a great deal of alcohol one night and was shouting abuse at the captain of the ferry which we could hear trundling away in the darkness. He declared to us all that he could swim the river and back twice in the time it took the ferry to do a one-way trip. Someone bet him five bob that he couldn't and there was a great splash as the sarge threw himself into the inky black water. We neither saw nor heard him again and he did not return to the castle that night. Some time on Sunday morning he returned to camp in a cheerful if dishevelled condition. He had been swept out of the mouth of the river in the pitch black night and carried eastwards along the coast by the tide and currents until in the pale light of dawn he had been cast up on the north-east coast of the island, and had more or less dried out of both alcohol and water on the long walk back. I have a feeling that if he had not been almost pickled with whisky when he went in he would never have been around to order us to 'get fell in' again.

I spent a number of days sitting on the high turret on the top of the round tower of the castle with a notebook, Bren gun and no ammunition. The idea, I believe, was to note down and report any enemy aircraft crossing the coast and to frighten the pilot by waving my empty gun in his direction. I doubt whether it was fear of being reported by me but no German aircraft showed up; and I was able to make interesting drawings of Portsmouth and Osborne House from my lofty observation post.

We moved to a camp on the cliffs above Folkestone and set up an observation post in the old lighthouse at the end of the barbed-wired pier while shells were being lobbed across the Channel into the town and harbour and our side was lobbing shells back. The only useful observation I remember making was of a cormorant sitting on a drifting baulk of timber near enough for me to make a fairly detailed sketch.

Our next stop was in Scotland where we got down to the serious business of invasion training in the lochs and along the east and west coasts. It was my first visit to Scotland, where the scenery was magnificent and the training tough, and whenever we were not up to our necks in cold water or fighting off millions of hungry gnats along the beaches, I tried to capture the scenery in my sketchbooks. I still have a few drawings which survived being soaked in both fresh and salt water and rather more from a brief and relatively peaceful interlude near to Dumfries, where the local people were inordinately kind to us.

Although we had no official knowledge of what was happening when we were moved south again early in 1944, it was clear that the great armada was being assembled and we were simply waiting for The Day. For no reason that I can think of, I was suddenly sent on a wireless course to Wandsworth College, London. It was the time of buzz bombs when thousands of people were listening to the sinister drone of approaching missiles and wondering whether they would go over or the engine would cut out suddenly and send them scuttling for shelter. On my twenty-first birthday I returned to our billet in a commandeered house on Clapham Common. My bed was on the third floor and I was just settling down to read my mail and unpack the rather beaten-up birthday cake my mother had sent me in a parcel when the dreaded rocket engine noise was heard approaching. I sat there waiting to judge whether it was going to pass overhead when it suddenly cut out and I went down four flights of stairs so fast that I was in the basement with everyone else when the rocket landed. When I went back upstairs the window by my bed had been blown out. It had buried my birthday cards and letters under splintered wood, glass and rubble and my mother's cake had more glass in it than currants. I could hardly grumble. My friends in the East Yorks had much worse to come on D-Day a few weeks later and many of them died on the beaches.

I was on the last stage of my wireless course at Long Eaton in Derbyshire when I happened to pick up a copy of *The Artist* magazine in the NAAFI club in Nottingham. It contained a correspondence column which invited readers to send in examples of their work for free criticism, so I sent off a small selection and was staggered by the reply. It said that although they could not afford to pay me any money they would like to publish some of the drawings. It said that I had talent and that they would help me after the war by putting me in touch with 'the right people'. I read and reread that scrap of paper, unable to believe my eyes. They were as good as their word, too, in that they did publish two drawings in their editorial and did not pay anything for them. But they had promised to launch me into the world of art after the war. It was better than being knighted and my feet hardly touched the ground even on route marches.

Writing Home By Norman Thelwell

NEVER FORGET NATURE

VAST numbers of students neglect the greatest aid to the mastery of art—nature. They visit local exhibitions and spend long periods there, in order to see how others have achieved their aims; they buy and borrow books in order to read all they can about art. Yet those same students, when they go out sketching, somehow seem to work like a camera does: they simply 'snap' what they see without really studying it.

If you set out to study nature seriously, you will learn more from such study than by any other means. Nothing can take the place of such study, nothing can give you knowledge of her moods and tempers, her character and her beauty except close study.

The art school and books can teach you all there is to know about handling tools, tone, harmony, composition, colour; but when it comes to applying the knowledge gained, nature alone can be your true guide.

The reason is, of course, that every individual sees nature differently; aims and ideas differ too. That is why you must go to nature and commune with her; not always with sketch-book or painting equipment, but sometimes without even a pencil. It is a question of close contact; a few hours spent in examination, observation, and the study of fleeting as well as stable effects, should teach you much.

So never neglect nature; get as near her as you can as often as you can. She will lead you along the straight path and give you the knowledge you must possess if good, sound paintings are to be created by you. (Ed.)

Receiving Orders by Wireless By Norman Thelwell

Editor: Harold Sawkins. The copyright of all articles, paintings and drawings is reserved. THE ARTIST is published mid-monthly by The Artist Publishing Company. Editorial and Advertising Offices are at 51, Piccadilly, London, W.1. Registered at the G.P.O. for transmission to Canada and Newfoundland by Magazine Post. Entered as Second Class matter, August 3rd, 1933, at the Post Office, New York, N.Y., under the Act of March 3rd, 1879 (Sec. 523 P.L. and R.). SUBSCRIPTION orders for THE ARTIST should be sent to The Artist Publishing Company, 51, Piccadilly, London, W.1. Price 2s. 6d. per copy; subscription, 30s. per annum; 15s. per half-year, post free. U.S.A. and Canada, $7.50 per annum.

Shortly after this I went along for a few evenings to Nottingham Art School, where I met another young student named Rhona. By chance she also lived near Long Eaton and we travelled back on the same bus. She was in the Land Army, working locally, and we spent as much time as possible together before I went abroad with the REME.

After years of training for the Normandy landings and some weeks fiddling with wireless sets, which I never understood, I was sent to India.

16   Port Said

Scraps from 'Port Said'
14203149
fepm N. Thelwell . ROJRM. R·E·M·E·
India Command

The voyage turned out to be very enjoyable. The weather was perfect, we met no enemy action and after we had picked up a batch of Italian prisoners at Port Said we had music as well as clear moonlit evenings all the way to Bombay. I was deeply affected by the teeming squalor and poverty of India, by the gentle friendliness of its people and by the striking colour and visual beauty of it all. We moved from place to place on the incredibly overcrowded railways, with no idea of our ultimate destination, and we wondered sometimes whether anyone else knew why we were there or where we were going. I never saw a military radio again.

Up to that point I had never thought in terms of humorous drawings apart from the rather trivial sketches I put into my letters home to fill the space when there was nothing new to write about. It was during one of those periods of boredom and inactivity which affect all service people from time to time that I was thumbing through a pocket magazine called *Victory* and felt that the cartoon ideas were rather poor and the drawings even worse. It was that little bird that sits on all our shoulders that said to me, 'If you're so clever why don't you do something better?' I found it wasn't quite that easy but I finally squeezed out three corny ideas, made three drawings to illustrate them and sent them to the editor. About ten days later I received a cheque for more rupees than I was earning in a month.

My whole life flashed before my eyes, as it had frequently done before when stepping off the ramps of assault craft. I had never known anyone who came by money except through grinding hard work or years of mindless boredom. Even though I had enjoyed doing hundreds of drawings and paintings in my life I had never come across anyone before who was willing to pay for them – not more than a few shillings anyway. And yet here was this cheque, not very big perhaps but the biggest one I'd ever earned. Was it some sort of message, I wondered. Yes it was; and it didn't go out of the other ear, either, for the truth is that, with wide variations, I've been doing the same thing ever since.

Our first Train Journey.   Bombay-

Native
women
washing in
buffalo pool

Bullock Carts
at Secunderabad
India
1945.

49

Shortly after I started contributing work to *Victory* magazine we were packed onto a train once more and sent on another long mystery tour. We were stretching our legs on the station platform at Poona when the news broke that the war was finally over. Secunderabad turned out to be our destination and we were billeted in tents on the racecourse. We had not been doing nothing there for long when we were invited to a party by the Nizam of Hyderabad. It was exciting news, for everyone knew that he was one of the richest men in the world. We were looking forward to being entertained in his magnificent palace and living like sultans for a day. We had visions of reclining on silk cushions, eating rare eastern delicacies and taking an occasional puff at a jewel-encrusted hubble-bubble pipe as the dancing girls swayed and gyrated for our delectation.

The party took place in a hot, dusty field around a wooden bandstand. We dined on a kind of a thin nameless gruel followed by plates of sandwiches while a group of men in western-style dress played boring western tunes on violins. There was no palace or female of any kind in sight. It was a bit of a let-down; but after the dreadful poverty we had seen since we arrived in India, it seemed right and we hoped that the Nizam was also eating thin gruel and using his wealth to help his fellow countrymen.

It was in the tented camp at Secunderabad that an unusual notice appeared on company orders. In effect it said: 'Any man with professional knowledge of magazine production should report to company office at 9.00 hours.' I had no such knowledge but reported at 9.00 hours on the dot and was conducted, hat off and at the double, before three high-ranking officers with scarlet bands and tabs everywhere.

'What experience have you had?' I was asked by the central presiding officer. I put three or four sketchbooks on the table before him without replying. It seemed to have had a mild shock value because he did not repeat the question but flicked through the pages, glanced at his fellow officers and passed the books along. 'Pack your kit,' he said. 'You're going to GHQ Delhi.' I had a sneaking suspicion that we might have been on the way to Burma at that time so it was one of the few orders I was ever given in the Army that was really welcome.

New Delhi lacked the tumbling, surging beauty and squalor of the old Indian cities but it had been designed by Sir Edwin Lutyens as the capital city of the British Raj and it had a clean, open elegance of its own.

I was promoted to sergeant and shown into a rather spartan office in the administrative buildings near to the Viceregal Lodge and told that a magazine for the Indian Electrical and Mechanical Engineers was to be produced in about a month. Knowing nothing about electronics, mechanics or magazine production I was a bit apprehensive at first but there were others there who did know about these things. My job was to be art editor; I didn't know much about that either but it is surprising how quickly one can learn when one is interested.

For the next fourteen months, until I returned to the UK, I found myself responsible for almost every detail of graphics in the magazine and it was valuable experience. I did technical drawings, illustrations, headings, strip cartoons of a technical nature, cover designs and even some of the advertising matter. As the war was then over there was time to do other things like drawings for Indian magazines as well as forces publications which paid for contributions. I was astonished one day to receive a letter from the commander-in-chief, Field Marshal Auchinleck, who asked me to design some new uniforms for the Indian Army. I knew nothing about that kind of work either but I did it anyway and he could not have been too disappointed with my ideas because later he asked me to design a flag for the Boys' Regiment Indian Armoured Corp. I still have his letter of thanks for the work dated 3 October 1946.

It was not possible to buy Christmas cards in
Delhi so in 1945 I produced two or three of these
for myself and there was a ready market for them
among the thousands of men waiting for
repatriation.

*A greetings card for the editorial office at Delhi and a more
general design*

It was in India that I had my second and most traumatic encounter with horses. In April 1946 I became due for a month's leave from Delhi and, keeping to the best traditions of British India, I left the baking plains for the hills. Naini Tal was a very beautiful place nestling in the core of an extinct volcano. The only flat area was the lake in the centre and about half of its encircling road. The other part of the road climbed steeply up a towering promontory called Dorothy's Seat and fell away again to the lake beyond. The road was a ledge cut into the face of the rock – very beautiful if one had a head for heights. Unless one enjoyed rock climbing the only sensible way to complete a circuit of the lake was to hire a horse and let it do the donkey work. At one end of the lake was a riding establishment which hired out the most cunning collection of horses in the whole of India. They were not in the least vicious – just cunning. The view from the highest point of the hill road was breathtakingly beautiful with the glittering water far below, the steep wooded side of the crater opposite dotted with houses and, above the crest, a panoramic view of the snow-covered Himalayas shining in the crystal clear air. My horse was well behaved as we plodded steadily upwards and the road was reasonably wide, though I kept as far as possible from the cliff edge.

By the time we arrived at the highest point I was at peace with the world. Without being asked, my horse stopped whilst I took in the view. Then before I knew what was happening he walked across the road and with his hooves only inches from the edge he looked down the sheer precipice to the lake far below. He spotted a small clump of grass growing in a crevice a foot or two below the ledge and, with his top lip flapping, he strained downwards to reach it. He was a very big horse and I confess to having felt dizzy when I climbed into the saddle at the lakeside, but this was different. My head was reeling. It seemed so unfair to die now that the war was over by falling over a cliff on horseback. I plucked feebly at the reins in an effort to raise my horse's head but he gave a counter-jerk and the reins flew out of my hands,

over his head and dangled in space.

I thought of leaping from the saddle but we were so near to the cliff edge that the least misjudgement would have been fatal. I thought of rolling backwards and risking falling on my head but my muscles had seized up. I won't go on. I haven't had the nightmares for a long time now and I don't want to trigger them off again.

After what seemed like an eternity he gave up the struggle to reach the grass, raised his head and turned back the way we had come. His hooves shot a shower of stones and dust over the edge as he set off at a cracking pace down the steep incline.

They showed no surprise at the stables when we cantered up in record time, from the wrong direction with reins hanging loose. They salaamed without a hint of a smirk at my dishevelled condition and loaded up another would-be equestrian who was waiting for a mount. There was a rumour circulating among the holidaying troops that no one had ever made it over Dorothy's Seat on horseback. I don't know whether it was true, but I never met anyone who had – and plenty tried.

Towards the end of my stay I had spent a pleasant day painting at the lakeside and was walking back to the billet which was about halfway up the opposite side of the crater. I was tired and looking forward to dinner as I passed the stables. It was going to be a tiring walk up the zig-zag hill road and on an impulse I asked for a horse to take me home. It was normal practice to hire a horse for a one-way journey because the stabling area was littered with little Indian boys, about seven or eight years old, who regularly set off at a brisk trot behind the mounted sahibs and brought the horse back when the rider had reached his destination, or fallen off on the way.

This horse was very slow and reluctant as we rounded the lake towards the lower end of the hill path. I thought he would never make it up the slope so I urged him into a trot to get some inertia. To my astonishment he broke into a full gallop as we hit the slope. There was no sheer cliff edge to worry about on that road and I think I would have

Water buffaloes cooling off.

retained some control had it not been for the hairpin bends about every few hundred yards. As it was I was still in the saddle as we approached the house where five or six assorted soldiery were taking cool drinks on the terrace. They rose in a body to cheer my spectacular arrival and the cheers changed to howls of derisive laughter as we swept past, round the next zig-zag and on up the mountain. It was not long before we reached the rim of the crater where the horse stopped with nostrils flaring and flanks heaving. The ground fell away beyond into miles of virgin jungle backed by the Himalaya range. Another pace forward and I would certainly have jumped for my life but the

horse seemed to have had enough. I managed to turn him for a leisurely descent but the road down must have seemed like heaven to him after his mad dash up it and, before I could do anything about it, we were going down faster than we came up.

We passed the balcony full of unfeeling comrades for the second time at breakneck speed, urged on by shrieks of laughter and wild cat-calls and raced on down until we reached the lakeside once more. The little Indian boy was sitting on a rock waiting for us. He was a lovely, patient child – no hint of derision on his angelic face as the horse slid to a halt. He walked away along the darkening lake road, a tiny figure followed meekly

Thelwell

MY BEARER
IRWIN STADIUM
NEW DELHI
INDIA. 1946

PRAMA RAM. परमाराम

*My charpoy in the tent
on Secunderabad racecourse.*

*It seemed incongruous to me to
have a personal servant or bearer
to attend to our daily needs.
Prama Ram was my bearer at
Irwin Stadium, New Delhi,
and this delightful old gentleman
took great care of my clothing
and kit. It was a privilege to have known him.*

at heel by the great horse as if it were a well trained gun dog.

When I finally staggered into the billet I was in no mood to face the delighted crowd. I got through to the bathroom without them noticing that the ski-trousers I was wearing had split right down the back seam and, mercifully, as they fastened tightly at the ankles they never knew that my 'drawers – cellular – army' had been torn into two separate pieces and half had slipped down inside each trouser leg. I reflected that even Cowper's John Gilpin had not suffered *that* indignity. I have often been asked what started me drawing demented equestrians on frenzied mounts and I've never been able to give a sensible answer; but I have a feeling that the Renshaw Hall psychiatrist could have supplied one.

I had never sold a drawing to a British magazine but Rhona wrote to say that if I sent some ideas home to her she would send them to magazines in the UK and see what happened, which she did. It was thus that *London Opinion* bought my first drawing to be published in this country and started an association which, when I returned home, continued for some years. Meanwhile, Geoff Lucy, a colleague from the Indian Army magazine, had been demobilised and rejoined *News Review* in London. He wrote suggesting that I produce a series of caricatures of the Indian and Pakistan leaders who were very much in the news at the time. It was a small commission but valuable in that it gave me some confidence in dealing with a set piece of work and was another connection with publications in Britain.

The first cartoon, sent home from India and published in the British magazine London Opinion.

'It's always the same when I take you anywhere – rush-rush-rush at the last minute.'

Viceroy Archibald Wavell helped
the Indians to whittle away his own powers.

Jai Prakash Narain
The Socialists packed their bags

*Caricatures sent home from India
and published in* News Review.

I returned to England in November 1946 just in time for what was described by many as the worst winter in living memory. It was certainly the worst in mine either before or since. The *Queen of Bermuda* arrived at the Mersey bar packed to the gunwales with 3,000 homesick troops who had been away for years. Hundreds of relatives filled the landing stages, some of whom had been waiting for three days. Unbelievably the anchor was dropped within sight of the Liver Birds and we were left swinging in the tideway. We could not hear what our relations were saying about it but half of Liverpool must have heard the protests from the troops in language which threatened to strip the paint off the ship.

We were still on board the next day and there was confusion everywhere. The liner *Franconia* was still dozing at the stage and the *Empire Brent*, which was due to sail across the Atlantic with a cargo of 600 GI brides and their 300 children, was held up because the young ladies had brought too much luggage. I swear it's true! The ship simply could not hold all their frocks, hats, lingerie and nappies and I still have the press cutting to prove it. So the argument went on while 3,000 homesick soldiers and their eager loved ones tapped their feet and waited.

When the girls were finally ready the ship moved out to frantic cheering and ran smack into a cattle boat newly arrived from Ireland, tipping its pitiful cargo into the river. I'm not surprised. Any man who has waited for his spouse to decide what she is willing to be seen dead in when going out for the evening will understand. After days of arguing with 600 brides about what they could or could not put in their luggage, the captain of the *Empire Brent* must have been near dementia. It is to his credit that he managed to get his ship out of the river at all, to say nothing of doing so without sinking the *Queen of Bermuda* as well.

I had been commendably strong-minded in resisting the temptation to load myself down with useless souvenirs and had sensibly, I thought, brought back only two fez hats which I had bought in a weak moment from a Bum Boat at Port Said on the way out. Fezzes are not easy items to cart about in one's military gear for long periods without getting rumpled. Miraculously, however, they were still in prime condition when we disembarked. Fearful that they might be crushed in the final dash into loved ones' arms, I had tied them by their tassels to the end of my kit bag. I was being scraped along the woodwork halfway down the gangway when I was struck on the back of the head by the sharp corner of a metal kitbox which continued in an arc and scythed my fezzes off their tassels and down, down, down into the surging muddy water between ship and shore. I wonder sometimes if they are still there, preserved in the mud like the *Mary Rose.* As they sank out of sight they marked the end of a period in my life and the end of the gangway marked the beginning of another.

As things turned out I need not have worried about my fez hats being crushed in my mother's arms for I didn't see her for another two days. I doubt whether any returning warrior touched the sleeve of a relative that day even if they managed to spot one in the milling crowds for we were marched straight across the landing-stage to the waiting trains. It was like a gigantic, triumphant football team being shepherded to the dressing-room through a morass of frantic supporters trying to thump them on the back. I picked out only one verbal exchange from the cacophony of noise.

'I've got y' scouse on the 'ob, Billy!'

'We threw Billy overboard, Missus. Can we 'ave 'is scouse?'

And the trains pulled out for York.

There was only one thing I felt fairly sure of on that journey: if I was going to look more deeply into the endearing lunacy of human behaviour I had come back to the right place.

Returning home on the troop-ship Queen of Bermuda.

4: BACK TO
THE DRAWING-BOARD

*Pier Head Buildings, Liverpool.
It was in this area of the city that,
as a junior clerk in 1940–1,
I delivered letters from our office
to other business premises nearby
and trembled as a fire watcher
on the office roof during the blitz.*

I was twenty-three years old and had never met a professional artist – nor many amateurs, for that matter. So, after a week at home, I decided it was time I cashed in my trump card and I set off for London with a folio of drawings and my precious letter from *The Artist*. The office was in Burlington Arcade in those days, next door to the Royal Academy, which seemed significant. I had never been into Burlington Arcade before and a glance at the prices of the goods in the shop windows boosted my feelings that I was about to enter the big time. The wooden staircase to the office was a disappointment. The boards felt loose and there was no light. I knocked politely on the door at the top but there was no reply so I went in.

*The great Liverpool painter George Stubbs
painted this picture of one of my remote ancestors,
the Rev. Robert Carter Thelwell of Redbourne Hall,
Lincolnshire, with his wife and daughter.
It is signed and dated 1776 and is now
in the Holburne Museum, Bath.*

The room was bare except for a few chairs round the walls and a table at which a girl of about sixteen was sitting with a typewriter.

'Yes?' she queried.

I proffered the five-inch-square letter which I had been holding in my hand since I entered Piccadilly.

'Er, I had this letter,' I said weakly.

She read it with an air of faint distaste. 'Yes?' she repeated, looking back at me.

'Er, well, I wondered if I might have a word with someone?'

She peered at the letter again. 'This letter's nearly three years old,' she said with her nose wrinkled.

'Yes, I know. I've . . . er . . . been away.'

She peered again. 'Are you Pete Thrumell?'

'No,' I said. 'That's Private and the name's Thelwell.'

'You didn't tell me it was private,' she said indignantly.

'No, the letter's not private but three years ago I was Private. That's not Pete, that's Pte which is short for Private.'

She rose nervously and made for the inner door. 'Have a seat,' she said as she disappeared.

I felt more like having a lie-down.

I think I knew right then that it wasn't going to be roses, roses all the way. But still, if they only handed me on to the influential people, as their letter had promised, that would be good enough for me. I could do without the frills. There wasn't a sound from behind the inner door and I began to think the young lady had hidden in a cupboard waiting for help to arrive, when a man in shirtsleeves and no tie came out. He was holding my letter between thumb and forefinger as if it was someone else's soiled handkerchief.

'Are you Pete Thrumwell?' he asked. 'Miss Quigley says you didn't tell her it was a private letter until she'd read it. She seems a bit upset.'

'Look, mate,' I said, 'I'm sure we can clear this up if I can have a word with the editor.'

'I am the editor,' he said.

'Oh well, sir,' I said, 'you remember publishing a couple of my rough sketches in your editorial about three years ago when I was a private in the East Yorkshire Regiment? Well, that's the letter you sent me at the time.'

'We publish a lot of drawings in three years, you know, Pete. What did you want me to do?' he asked.

'Well,' I said, 'I just happened to be passing and I wondered if you could recommend a good place for me to get a sandwich and a cup of tea? I haven't had a bite since breakfast.' He was very helpful but when I got outside I went to the nearest pub.

I don't think my mother was the least bit surprised when I arrived home the next day. She had read the letter from *The Artist* long ago and didn't seem very impressed. She didn't ask about London and I was grateful.

There were tens of thousands of men and women in the same situation in 1947 and more coming home every week. Many of us had not had the opportunity of going on to college because of call-up so there was a government scheme which offered subsistence grants to those who wished to continue their education after demobilisation. It seemed a good idea to find out a bit more about being an artist before risking another interview with a London typist, so I went to Liverpool College of Art for a degree course.

For the first time in my life I spent time among

Busts in the sculpture room at Liverpool College of Art 1948.

people who did not equate scribbling on paper with the early signs of mental disintegration. There were two main groups of students, the ex-service people – mainly men in their early twenties – and a younger stratum of boys and girls who had come straight from their previous schools. It was a good mix which worked very well but there were some difficulties, particularly during that winter of 1946–7. For example, everything was still rationed and it was almost impossible to get sweets, cigarettes or other luxuries of the kind without much winking, nose-tapping and elbows in the ribs. No doubt present-day experts would say that we were lucky not to get them easily; but it was difficult to get clothing, too, and nearly impossible to get coal or fuel of any kind. The upshot was that, as the snow continued to fall and freeze, fall again and freeze again in a seemingly endless cycle, I began to wonder why I had been in such a hurry to get home from India. It was a steady climb from Liverpool Central station to the college and, without spiked shoes, one had to cling to the walls or railings to avoid sliding back down to the station. It was like climbing the north face of the Eiger on roller skates.

Schools and other large public buildings ran out of fuel so that we sat at our drawing-boards in macs and top coats and tried to draw with gloves on. I was deeply sorry for the models who posed for us clad only in goose pimples, nicely textured though they often were. Due to exigencies of the times it was possible to complete the normal five-year degree course in three years, provided that the intermediate and national diplomas could be obtained in one year each instead of the normal two with an additional year for the Art Teachers' Diploma. Most of the ex-service students felt that they were already well behind in their chosen careers – some were already married – so that there was a feeling of genuine urgency and we certainly worked very hard during the day and most evenings we were required to complete projects for criticism at a general assembly the next day. I confess to being astonished at how many subjects had to be studied for the diplomas in addition to the obvious drawing and painting. We studied sculpture, the history of painting, illustration, architecture, furniture and costume, in addition to a number of crafts such as lithography, engraving, etching, pottery, etc. It was a very full programme and we were often very tired by the time we arrived home.

In view of my own ignorance of the number of subjects taught at art schools it is not surprising that the general public had no idea either and the fact was nicely expressed by the gentleman who lived next door. I was returning home at 6.30 p.m. on a pleasant summer evening when I passed him leaning on his front gate. I had a painting for the college to do that evening and a drawing for *London Opinion* before I went to bed; I had been up until 3 a.m. that morning working on another job. He gave me a knowing smile. 'Been wrestling with a pencil all day have we, son?' he laughed. But I was too tired to enlighten him.

My life at school and in the forces had not been particularly enjoyable so that my three years at Liverpool College were bound to be a relief by comparison and it was a time which I would not have missed. I learned a great deal from daily

Student work at Liverpool College of Art:
(left) scraper-board design for an article on English canals;
(right) wood-engraving from a sketch of
Normanton Church, Derbyshire.

Another art school exercise: design for a decorative panel.

contact with my fellow students and their work as well as from members of the teaching staff; and the technical facilities of the printing department were particularly useful. I enjoyed working with almost all kinds of artists' materials but was never very happy with Indian ink. This dense black ink is waterproof when dry and cannot be smudged, so it is very suitable for making black-and-white drawings for reproduction. It tends to clog on the pen nib very quickly, however, and this interferes with the freedom of line-drawing. I would have avoided using it had it not been for the fact that I had been told that magazine editors would accept nothing else. So I persevered with it for years, hating it more and more until I found myself regarding Indian ink bottles as if they contained acid.

I was on my way home from college in a crowded bus one winter evening and was jammed tightly against the window by a huge lady who occupied about three-quarters of the double seat. It was dark and pouring with rain outside and we were all soaking wet. I was so tightly confined that I could hardly move my arms and my least attempt to do so made the lady glare at me as if she thought I was either an unbearable fidget or being far too familiar. It was difficult to breathe without a disapproving glance, and every lurch of the bus

was making things worse, when I became aware of something trickling down my left leg. I had felt no sharp pain so it could hardly have been blood, but it was certainly something nasty and I was determined to find out what. I managed to work my left hand through my mac pocket, ease my jacket out of the way and locate my trouser pocket while the lady glared and hissed and grunted as if they were her pockets I was exploring. There was no going back; I had to find out what was happening and, with a final effort, my hand slid through into some dreadful liquid. I pulled it out again in panic and looked at my hand. It was jet black and shining wet. My travelling companion gave a strangled squeak and, pushing aside standing passengers, moved away down the bus. I put my hand back into my mac pocket and kept it there until I got home. Every item of my clothing except my right sock was ruined beyond hope and had to be replaced. I thanked heaven that I was wearing black shoes. I must have put the bottle in my pocket without tightening the screw cap. It was only a small bottle of Indian ink but very expensive.

After the rigid pecking order of the forces I was surprised to find that art schools, too, had their own system of class distinction and prejudice. This had nothing to do with origins or background, nor was it concerned with knowledge, skill or experience; it hung entirely upon the name of the particular course which one chose to follow. At the top of the order were the 'Fine Art' students – mainly the painters in oils; the sculptors were a small rarefied group with all-over dandruff and charisma; 'Commercial Arts' students, which included book illustrators and designers, were a sub-species; and those who toyed about with crafts were more or less outcasts.

Although there was a tendency for enclaves to form from time to time, it is true to say that the members of the various groups mixed freely enough, particularly in the hurly-burly of the students' common room, but the foolish distinctions pervaded the college and when I later became a teacher (or was I a lecturer?) at another college of art I found that the same attitudes prevailed, even to some extent among the staff. In my nine years as a full-time student and teacher in art schools it was the one and only aspect which I disliked, not because individuals were deeply affected by it but because it seemed to diminish artists in general and the colleges in particular. As among all human beings, the abilities of art students (and teachers) vary widely and I have never noticed that the quality of the work they produced had any direct bearing on whether a person bore the label 'Fine Artist' or 'Commercial Artist'.

In retrospect I think that many of us learned more in the delicious overcrowded common rooms than we did in our set studies and I have a suspicion that this may have been due to the fact that attitudes to the study of art seemed bereft of humour while the common rooms often rocked with music and laughter and the pure enjoyment of life. Whatever the reason, almost all the memorable moments for me are connected with break-time and lunch hours.

There was the lady who had been posing in the nude for us all morning and who joined us (fully dressed) at the long table where we were having lunch. Nylon stockings had only recently been introduced and were very scarce. She startled us all by suddenly throwing a large and shapely leg onto the table with such a crash that our plates leapt into the air.

'What do you think of *that?*' she demanded.

We wiped the gravy off our faces and made suitable noises of appreciation. She left the leg in place and surveyed it with obvious satisfaction whilst we gathered round for a closer inspection.

'That – is – a – beaut, Sybil!' said Frank, leaning very close and screwing an imaginary jeweller's eyeglass into his eye. 'That – is – a – real – hum – dinger and no mistake.'

'Not my leg, you idiot,' she shouted. 'The nylons. They're sheer.'

'So they are,' said Frank, touching her ankle gingerly with his forefinger. 'Just have a feel of this, lads,' he said, running his finger along her shin bone.

He was several inches short of her knee when Sybil's handbag caught him behind the head and sent him sprawling. She removed her leg, smoothed her skirt, patted her hair and stalked out in high dudgeon to prepare for the afternoon pose.

'Leave your nylons on, Sybil,' said a student near the door, avoiding her handbag by inches. But she never did.

It is not very often that ordinary life throws up humorous situations which are rich in content, perfect in build-up and exquisite in timing; but they happened in that common room with amazing frequency. When fuel became available there was often a big open fire at one end of the room and keen competition to bag one of the chairs which clustered round it. There was a young student called Dicky who had an unfortunate affliction of the skin which necessitated his hands being constantly enveloped in bandages. Anyone who has ever worn a small plaster on an injured finger will know how difficult it is to keep such things scrupulously clean and wholesome when working. Dicky often had to work with ink, paint, charcoal or modelling clay, all of which have a natural affinity for bandages. We were clustered round the fire in a noisy semicircle when Dicky extracted an orange from his jacket pocket and began to peel it. As his bandages were bulky and allowed only about two inches of his fingers to emerge, it was a task which required every ounce of concentration. Unfortunately it was one of those thin-skinned oranges which seem to contain about four times their own volume of juice under pressure and the instant that he penetrated the peel the juices oozed out. It was only the absorbent quality of his bandages that prevented it from dripping off his elbows. So complete was his concentration that he was quite unaware of the deathly silence which had fallen and the looks of stark horror which masked the faces of his friends as he continued to torture and mutilate the unyielding fruit. It seemed an age before the plucky orange gave up and a soggy lump of pulp lay helpless on the saturated bandages. He looked round at the wide-eyed faces beside him and said, 'Would anybody like a slice?'

While I was a student at Liverpool I began selling more and more drawings to various magazines, most of which contained some element of humour; and yet I tried it only once in the work I produced at college, with such disastrous results that I never dared to attempt it again. The subject was a 'Hill Farm' to be treated in any medium or manner the student chose. I chose on that occasion to treat it humorously and I worked very hard at the task. The picture consisted mainly of sheep, horses, pigs and chickens tearing madly about an extremely hilly farm while the farmer tore about after them trying to bring them all to heel. The whole thing was treated in a fairly realistic manner and the exaggerations were mainly in the movement rather than in the form. I realise in retrospect that it was a forerunner of the sporting prints which I developed some years later. My picture was put on the wall along with all the rest for the criticism session which was conducted by a member of staff who had always treated my work with fairness and consideration in the past. On this occasion he gave it a cursory glance, tapped it with his knuckle and said, 'Any fool can produce that kind of stuff,' and moved on.

Although Britain has in the past been rather less inclined to honour its own painters than most other European countries, it has produced a long line of cartoonists, caricaturists and humorous artists from Hogarth onward, whose genius has been recognised and applauded here at home as well as overseas. Furthermore, I have found that artists in general enjoy humour at least as much as any other human beings and most of those I have met seemed to have retained the attractive irresponsibility of youth rather longer than most. I find it difficult, therefore, to understand why the introduction of humour into picture-making has been regarded with such suspicion and embarrassment in our art schools. The work of Eric Revillious and Edward Bawden is full of delicious humour which exactly complements their exquisite sense of pattern and design; as indeed it adds delight to the very English wood-engravings of Thomas Bewick.

It is the ability to laugh which does as much as anything to distinguish *Homo sapiens* from the rest of animal creation. A sense of humour is, after all, a sense of proportion and hatred and bitterness cannot live with it. Satire is an important weapon against human folly and excess and I cannot see why art schools tend to freeze humour and satire out of their brief. It is in no way an isolated or inward-looking form of visual art; indeed it embraces every other branch without exception. A study of the great men such as Pieter Bruegel, Hogarth, Gilray, Daumier, Rowlandson, and many others since their day, shows their masterly handling of figure and animal subjects as well as landscape and architecture in a rich variety of mediums.

I am not suggesting that 'Humorous Art' should necessarily be taught as a separate subject but that students who show a natural aptitude or distinct talent for it should be given every encouragement to develop their skills and not be made to feel that it is an inferior occupation to pouring tins of paint over acres of good canvas and then rolling in it.

*Wet Day at Woodchurch. This water-colour sketch
was made in 1948 during a students' outdoor painting session.
The teacher did not turn up and neither did any other students –
and I don't blame them.*

Come to think of it, humour in art would be very
difficult to teach to anyone who does not have an
inborn flair for it. But then, so is every other form
of art – as I quickly discovered when I started my
year as a student teacher in 1949–50. It was the
final year of my degree course.

We had been well saturated with the various
theories of how to impart artistic knowledge to
others when I went forth to practise spreading the
message to the masses. I decided to go back to my
old infants' school where Frank Smith had
enriched my vocabulary and the air-ship R101 had
changed the course of art, twenty-two years before.
What better place was there to start my
student-teacher year?

It was a nostalgic experience to enter the same classroom again and see all the bright little children sitting quietly at our old desks with their arms folded and their mouths shut. The white sausages had long gone from the walls and the theories of Froebel and Marion Richardson had got there before me. I could tell that because the desks were still the same size as before but the pieces of paper that lay on them were so big that they hung over the sides and, in some cases, were supported upon the heads of the children in front. There were no chalks, but each child was supplied with a two-pound jamjar of water, several cocoa tins of powdered colour and a brush so large that in the restricted confines of the screwed-down desks they protruded some distance over their shoulders when the infants took them in hand. There was no room on the desks for any of this hardware so it was placed on top of the paper.

Miss Birchinall, the teacher, was an utterly charming little woman. After introducing me to the class, who startled me by chanting, 'Good morning sir', she said she was sure that I was anxious to get on and quietly departed. The bead curtain on the glass panel of the door had scarcely settled into silence when all hell broke loose. It was not so much the noise that threw me but the fact that every child in the room left its seat and scurried hither and thither about the place like disturbed ants. They not only ignored my pleas for order but appeared not to hear or even see me. Indeed, it was only their lack of size and weight that saved me from being borne down and trampled. They had brought their brushes with them and were plunging them into any jamjar or cocoa tin they came across and daubing great gobs of colour in the general direction of any paper which came to hand. At times there were five or six of them stabbing at one piece of paper, like pygmies trying to kill a wild pig. A water jar went over and two little girls were trying to wring out their dresses. One little boy (who was sitting at his own desk) received a two-pound jamjar of water over his head from the tier of desks behind him and kept following me about trailing water, pointing vaguely

and saying, 'He done it – he done it!' I was at my wits' end.

This was the kind of situation I was now expected to cope with, however, and I knew that whatever else I did I must not show fear. I did have some temporary success by waving my arms about and rushing at them. About half the herd broke and fled into a corner where they all tried to get into one desk. Several more jars of water went over and some tins of powder colour fell onto the floor and went off like coloured smoke-bombs. When I looked round, the other lot were in an eager semi-circle behind me waiting to see what I was going to do to those I had trapped.

Perhaps it was the beads of sweat on my forehead that scared them. It certainly wasn't my paint-spattered clothing, because theirs was just as bad, but, whatever the reason, they scuttled away to the opposite corner. They were at least all now in the desk area and I had the teacher's bit of the floor to myself. I found that by crouching like a sheepdog and watching them keenly with narrowed unwavering eyes I was beginning to gain control. Nearly half an hour had gone by and I hadn't started to teach them yet. The room was a shambles and my hands were shaking. One little boy (looking horribly like Frank Smith) walked towards me with his brush, placed it on the floor and stood on his head. That was it! I would have to use psychology on him: get to know the kid and find out what made him tick. He fell right over onto his back so, keeping my foot under tight control, I helped him up with my hand. I crouched down, gave him a friendly smile and said, 'What's *your* name, sunshine?' He picked up his brush and flicked it. The paint struck me between the eyes and trickled down my face. To be fair to those children not one of them laughed. They just stared at me as if I was crazy.

When the door knob rattled it wasn't very loud but the effect was magical. Every child was back in a seat in seconds with arms folded. The only sound was of dripping water and a jamjar rolling under a desk. Miss Birchinall ignored the paint dripping off my chin.

'They look as if they've had a good time,' she said.

'Have you enjoyed your lesson, children?'

'Yes, Miss Birchinall.'

'And what do we say? Thank – you – Mister – Thelwell.'

'Thank you Mister Thelwell,' they chanted.

If ever you read this book, Miss Birchinall, thank *you*. You were a brick.

It required all my self-control to avoid running until I got outside the school gate and when I reached safety I ticked 'infant teaching' off my list. I decided to deal with my second scheduled visit by stuffing cotton-wool up my nose, ringing the headmistress and claiming to have gone down with 'flu. I was prepared to join a 'More pay for infant teachers' march any time.

'What a lovely idea Miss Peebles!
A lesson on poster design for the art class!'

Cartoon for the *News Chronicle*, 1959.

My next assignment as a student pedagogue was to bring art to one of the new comprehensive schools – which was much easier. This easing of my problems reflected no particular credit on either me or my students but was due entirely to Mr Lunt, the encumbent part-time art teacher who also dealt with religious instruction and physical training. Boxing was his particular interest. He was a cheerful, thick-set man of about forty and he had an enviable knack of combining any or all of his specialist subjects in one lesson when he thought it necessary. He took one look at me and never left me alone with the class again. Luckily, his own knowledge and ability in the field of visual art was sketchy, if not entirely absent, and with him sitting discreetly in a corner pretending to mark exercise books, I was free from disciplinary problems. Indeed, Mr Lunt (call me Albert) and I hit it off so well that we became a sort of educational double-act and I spent more time in his class than my own assignment strictly demanded. Albert asked me if I had any objection to him knocking a bit of religion into their fat heads for a few minutes each session before I got onto the art lark.

'They'll be damn glad to listen to you when I've finished with 'em,' he promised.

Albert had a magic touch which was sometimes delivered with the flat side of his prayer book if he spotted any lad with his eyes open whilst he was calling upon heaven to forgive their sins. He would open the Bible at random and read a passage or two in stentorian tones which must have been audible three classrooms away, thumping the nearest desk with his fist like an evangelist in a city of sin.

'And the Lord spake unto Moses saying – Ainsworth! Do I have to spake unto *you*, lad? You'll think *you're* wandering in the desert if I do. And the Lord spake unto Moses saying . . .' It was rich stuff and it was an agony trying not to laugh.

I did a spell also with evening-class students – no self-preservation worries there. So peaceful, it was like a Sunday morning in Birkenhead before the Boys' Brigade started up.

It is not only present-day parents who think that their children have taken leave of their senses. My own parents thought that I had, for in April of 1949, Rhona and I decided to get married during the end of term break. It was thanks to a couple of drawings for *London Opinion*, *Men Only* (not a 'girlie' magazine in those days) and two or three decorations for *Everybody's Weekly* that we spent our honeymoon at the Red Lion in Clovelly. I'm not sure why but when we both returned with a supply of drawings of the place – some by Rhona and some by me – there were a number of friends who swore we had prepared them before we went.

At the end of the degree course in 1950 we were required to put on a general exhibition of all our work in addition to submitting the usual written thesis. I had had a sudden rush of blood to the head some months before and purchased half of a rather elderly Austin Seven Ruby. The other half was bought by my mother and it cost us sixty pounds in all. I will never forget the moment when it was delivered by a salesman who arrived in a long, low, sleek Jaguar which was parked smack outside the front gate. My mother, who didn't know an Austin Ruby from Stephenson's rocket, rushed out, threw her hands up, beaming with pleasure, and breathed, 'It's lovely, Norm – it's lovely!' She was so enraptured that as she leaned over the gate she didn't even notice the Austin parked behind it. It was a sad moment when I was forced to screw her head round gently and point to our own vehicle. 'You don't mean . . . you don't mean . . . that?' she said. 'It looks like a bassinet. I pushed you and Alan round in a better pram than that,' she added, '*and* it had a better polish.' Our son, David, was born just in time for me to pick him and Rhona up from the hospital and take them home by car.

Well, as I said, we had to put on this exhibition of three years' work at Liverpool and the material was heavy. It included sculpture (no stone, but plaster casts can be heavy enough) and the problem was how to get it all across the river from

Birkenhead. I had failed my first driving test in the Ruby because none of the friends who volunteered to accompany me on practice runs had ever told me that once the clutch was let out it was possible to control the speed of the car by depressing it part of the way down when moving in low gear. The consequence was that the car tended to leap forward when we moved off and backing into a narrow space became a hit-and-miss affair. I knew I'd failed when I backed into a back entry without contacting the clutch and ending up so tightly wedged against someone's backyard wall that it took me, the driving examiner and a surprised passer-by all our strength to extricate the back bumper from between two bricks. It's true that he marked a ridiculous number of other points as contributing to my failure but I think that was just temper.

It happened, however, that my second driving test was due on the morning when I had to get my artistic achievements over the river. My prayers were answered when the examiner turned out to be a new and much more even-tempered man. I passed, if not with flying colours, at least with only a friendly warning to get a few things on the car 'looked at' including the starter motor. It couldn't have worked out more conveniently. In the afternoon I crammed everything into the back seat – which took some time – and set off for the Mersey Tunnel. Unfortunately it was just about five in the afternoon when I got to the entrance. For anyone who has never driven through the Mersey Tunnel, I would advise them never to do so at about five o'clock in the afternoon for this is when everyone in Liverpool is driving back to Birkenhead and everyone in Birkenhead is returning to Liverpool, and about three quarters of them drive heavy lorries. The last time I had entered that underground engineering wonder was when I walked through it holding my uncle's hand the day before it was opened to traffic – and it frightened me then. On this occasion it was so dark between the huge lorries that I thought I'd gone blind. The light on the dashboard didn't work so I couldn't see the instruments. The lights overhead flashed down between the lorries, on, off, on, off, at one-second intervals until I was as dazed as a drunk in a disco hall – and the noise was even worse. The roar of the traffic was so loud that I couldn't hear my own engine and was terrified that it had cut out. I was convinced for a time that it was the lorry behind that was pushing me along.

However, it was not until I got to the Liverpool end that the real trouble started. You come out of the tunnel, if you are lucky, onto what I think is

This cartoon appeared in the News Chronicle *when the first stretch of the new motorway was opened in 1958.*

called St George's Plateau. It is a wide open area where about thirty main roads converge and a lone policeman stands in the centre and sorts out the mess. Well, that's what it was like in 1950 and it was just as the lorry in front swung away to freedom that the policeman turned and stopped our line of traffic. I slammed on the brake and the engine stalled. The road takes an upward slope as it emerges and the Ruby started to roll slowly backward down the tunnel. I skinned my knuckles getting the handbrake on hard enough to hold us before we hit the lorry behind. Then the engine wouldn't restart. I knew that any minute the policeman would call me on and the sweat began popping from the pores. I flogged the starter button without remorse but not a dicky-bird. The policeman looked my way and beckoned me forward but all I could do was keep my foot hard down on the footbrake in case the handbrake wires snapped, and keep flogging the starter. I could hear the battery getting fed up. When I didn't move at the policeman's behest an ear-splitting cacophony of blaring motorhorns almost blew the canvas top off the car. Even through that noise I could hear some of the dreadful names the lorry driver behind was calling me. The policeman got fed up and called on other lines of traffic. The perspiration was flowing freely as the battery was

getting weaker. Once more the policeman called me on. I stuck my head out of the window and shouted to the lorry driver that I was doing all I could to start the thing but she just wouldn't have it. When he started to climb down from his cab I would have abandoned the car and all its contents if I could have escaped. By now there were two miles of motorhorns and curses blasting out of the tunnel entrance and the policeman abandoned the rest of the traffic and walked across to find out what I was messing about at. I was glad to see him coming because although I had managed to slam the window up before he could get his hands on me, the lorry driver was glaring through the glass, banging on the canvas top and mouthing words which I didn't want to hear. I waited until the law took charge before lowering the window again.

'What's going on here, sir?' asked the policeman, running his eyes over my car.

'The engine's stalled, constable,' I said, 'and she just won't start.'

'May I see your licence, sir?'

I fumbled in my pocket and handed him my little red book. Several more drivers had emerged from the tunnel and were standing round the car. I couldn't see out of the windows for work clothes and hairy fists. The policeman glanced at the licence and did a double-take.

'Henry! Henry! You mad fool! Let him overtake!'

'This was only issued today,' he said, his face screwed up in disbelief. 'When did you pass your driving test?'

'This morning,' I said.

'Gawd strewth,' said someone.

'And you decided to drive through here at rush-hour in this vehicle?' he said with his hand clapped to his forehead.

'The loony's got a nude bird in the back,' said one of the drivers, peering through the glass at my sculptural exhibit. Faces appeared at every window.

'Let's get this heap off the road,' said another.

The policeman gave them a nod and they all bent down in unison, picked up the car with me and my nude bird in it and dropped it (unnecessarily hard I thought) against the left-hand wall.

The traffic roared past me a few moments later like water from an unblocked drainpipe. The policeman gave me my licence back.

'Give her a few minutes' rest and she'll probably start,' he said. 'I expect you've flooded her,' and he went back to his point duty.

I sat tight for nearly ten minutes saying the Lord's prayer over and over – and it worked. Ruby roared into life at the first touch and we went round the constable like a rocket. I was unloading my exhibition outside the college ten minutes later. The salesman had promised me she was a good little runner.

We left Liverpool and Birkenhead that summer of 1950 and, having acquired a post to teach design and illustration at Wolverhampton College of Art, there was a lot of buzzing about to do finding a house and settling in before the opening of the autumn term. The Austin did sterling duty carrying things back and forth to the semi we had acquired on the outskirts of the town, but only in short bursts. It turned out to be a surprisingly pretty journey through Whitchurch and Newport; which was a mercy because we never knew how much of the distance Ruby would be prepared to cover on any particular day, and we often had to spend long periods waiting for help to arrive. She had the habit of 'stripping cogs' suddenly when we were miles from anywhere. At least, that's what the garage men said she was doing. I hadn't realised that an Austin Seven had so many cogs to strip.

A drawing from my motoring book, Belt Up

She was bad on her wheels, too, even in a light crosswind, and would develop alarming wobbles just when we felt we might make it the whole way. We felt we knew almost every tree on that seventy-mile journey because we seemed to have broken down near every one of them at one time or another and we frequently had to get home by train.

When the time came for our final departure we left the car for my mother, who was determined that my father would learn to drive, come hell or high water, so that they would be able to 'get about a bit' when we had gone. After all, she did own half of it. The job of teaching him fell to my brother Alan, since I was no longer there to take my share of the risk, and I thanked heaven for it. Poor Alan aged five years in the next six months and developed a twitch. It was not that my father was nervous of the car, or any other traffic for that matter; on the contrary, he loved every moment when he was behind the wheel and was totally confident. The trouble was that he was convinced that all he had to do was to start the car and then steer it round and between things without hitting them. The last vehicle he had driven was a wooden box on old pram-wheels when he was a child and, as far as he was concerned, the Austin was just a posher version of the same thing. He expected everyone to leap out of the way when they saw him coming. He never did cotton on to which pedal did what and when a passenger shrieked and tried to get under the seat he would stab at any or all of the pedals at once and just concentrate on trying to miss whatever was bearing down on him.

Now when I met my brother he had no time for a friendly greeting; he would grab me by the lapels and shout: 'Oh my God! Do you know what he did last Saturday? We came round the corner into Grove Road at about forty miles an hour. You know, where the buses load up on both sides of the road. Well, there was a double-decker on each side and not enough space between them to get a bike through. I yelled for him to stop but he must have stamped on the accelerator. I swear to you that he went through at about forty-five and picked up blue paint from both buses without turning a hair . . . It can't go on Norm! It can't go on! I've got to think of Kath and the children.'

Or, 'Did you hear what happened on the Sunday? I must have been mad to take him out. I was still shaking from the double-decker business. I took him up Levers New Road – you know, away from the traffic – and he was batting along nicely when I told him to turn left into Snakes Lane when we came to it. I kept telling him to slow down but he wouldn't and as we got nearer I told him to abandon the turn and keep straight on but it was too late. He swung the wheel over as we came level, shot straight across the lane, up the grass bank, through the hedge and into the field. I'd hardly had time to brace my feet against the dashboard when the engine packed up trying to cross the ploughed land. The worst of it was,' he added, 'all Dad said was, "She doesn't seem to steer very well"!'

In the end Alan bought the car to save lives and with his careful handling it survived for another year or two before the final *coup de grâce*. The Ruby was what is known, I believe, as a cabriole, which meant that the roof was made of canvas and, if anyone was fool enough to try, it could be rolled backwards and strapped down so that back-seat passengers could have their hair ripped out at the roots by the wind. Alan parked it outside his house and one day a young cyclist getting healthy exercise on a racing bike came along the road with his head well down and his legs going like pistons. He didn't see the car until he hit the back bumper. He was catapulted over the handlebars and through the rear of the car and, collecting canvas as he went, ended upside-down in the front seat. Luckily, he was small and wiry, like my father and, like him, didn't get excited over trivial matters. When Alan pulled him out he said he was very sorry but just didn't notice the car. He hoped the damage wasn't serious and walked away with what was left of his racing model draped over his shoulder.

My father never did learn to drive but he was a jolly good singer and one can't have everything.

(above and right) Life and character drawings from student days at Liverpool.

5: 'WANT ME IN THE RUDE, DEARY?'

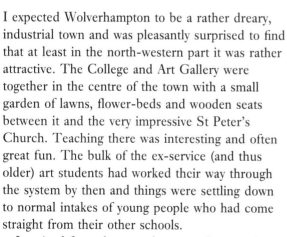

I expected Wolverhampton to be a rather dreary, industrial town and was pleasantly surprised to find that at least in the north-western part it was rather attractive. The College and Art Gallery were together in the centre of the town with a small garden of lawns, flower-beds and wooden seats between it and the very impressive St Peter's Church. Teaching there was interesting and often great fun. The bulk of the ex-service (and thus older) art students had worked their way through the system by then and things were settling down to normal intakes of young people who had come straight from their other schools.

I noticed from the start that, as at Liverpool, there were usually a number of quite talented musicians among each intake of art students and their common room, although smaller, was as lively and noisy as the one I had left. I'm not knowledgeable about pop music but I think we were moving into the age of skiffle, because

washboards and tea-chest-double-basses were much in evidence. It must have been alarming for musical instrument manufacturers to see young people going over to ironmongery. The students had a piano in their common room which had lost most of its woodwork and what was left kept falling off from time to time due to the vibration of the honky-tonk music which they beat out of it. Later the entire instrument disintegrated during a particularly hotted-up session.

As it happened we were able to help them out. My mother had bought a pianola at a sale at the beginning of the war and it was her pride and joy: not because she ever played it, but because the woodwork was huge and exquisitely polished and my mother's hobby was polishing furniture and trying to get my father to do the same. The instrument must have weighed about two tons. Alan and I had both been sent to piano lessons when we were young, which had been an abortive operation, but we could both pedal a pretty good tune out of the pianola when we had nothing else to do. My mother squeezed a note or two out of it from time to time but always noticed a finger mark and went over to polishing again. My father treated it exactly the same as he did the Austin Ruby and had the same trouble with the pedals. My Uncle

Johnnie, however, who was a bachelor and lived with us, spent many a Sunday afternoon giving 'The Entry of the Boyards' or 'The Prelude to Zampa' the full treatment with the loud lever at full throttle. The whole house vibrated until we wished the bellows would explode.

By the time we had settled down in our Wolverhampton semi (it had semi-sized rooms, too) we had more or less forgotten about the pianola until Rhona and I returned there one day and found it standing on the gravel path just inside the front gate. It was like running into a horse in the bathroom. It was in working order, too. I tried it and discovered the 'Prelude to Zampa' was still inside the trapdoor, but it brought the neighbours out *instanter* and it was maddening trying to explain that I didn't know how it had got there. Anyone who has ever tried pushing a two-ton pianola on castors through four inches of gravel chippings will understand our dilemma. It wouldn't budge an inch and we couldn't get the car past it. So the car stayed outside on the road and the pianola stayed inside on the path. It stayed there for three days, in fact, before we could recruit enough labour to move it. When we did we found it was too big to go through the front door and it had to be trundled and levered all the way round the back and in through the french door of the living room. Unfortunately, the living room was tiny and the pianola was huge so we had to shift most of the living-room furniture into the kitchen to make space for it, which made washing up difficult and washdays a nightmare. The instrument so dominated the room that we couldn't bear to go in it any longer and abandoned it until we could locate a pianola technician who could take the wretched thing apart and transfer it bit by bit to the slightly larger sitting room at the front of the house. When we did find such an expert the operation turned out to be protracted and expensive and it didn't help our peace of mind to realise that when the pianola was reassembled it became a permanent fixture until someone employed another specialist to take it apart again and heave the pieces through the window. It was

the first piece of 'built-in' furniture we ever owned.

In case anyone is wondering, my mother told us later that she had met a man who was driving down to Wolverhampton to pick up a load of furniture and, on an impulse, had asked him if he would drop the pianola off at our house because she knew that we hadn't had time to acquire any really nice furniture of our own.

This, then, was the situation the day that I heard an almighty crash from the students' common room and realised that their piano had finally fallen apart. I walked in, feeling like Elton John offering to rescue Watford Football team, and told the students, who were trying to play the framework like a harp, that I would give them a huge and beautiful new instrument if they would care to collect it. They cared.

It was winter, I remember, just a few days before Christmas when they turned up to collect it. They had pushed a flat trolley with six-inch diameter wheels about four miles through the snow which was still falling, and they poured into the house like ants invading a pantry. I remember about eight but Rhona says there were fifteen of them – and she should know, because they were still dismembering the thing by lunch-time and she went out to buy fish and chips for them all while I stayed behind to make sure that they dismembered only the pianola.

With most of the 'innards' out, the frame of the instrument was still the same size; and how they got it out of the house without taking the frame of the front door with them I do not know, but they did and the whole crowd set off down the road as if it was students' rag day. Somehow one of them was managing to beat a tune out of it as they went.

It took us some time to clear up the debris because they had decided they only wanted the piano and had torn out the pianola mechanism before departing. It had had more tubing inside it than the average cow so that our front room looked like a slaughter house. When the dustman came to collect it all, he asked me if I'd got rid of my mother-in-law and I had to give him a tip to keep his voice down. The piano was still beating out break-time music three years later but the students never did put all the woodwork back on it and I often wondered how long it survived before there was another almighty crash.

In spite of having unloaded the pianola on the art students and thus restored our semi to its original capacity, we soon moved to a new abode in the nearby village of Codsall where we had a little more elbow room, at least outside. Inside it made very little difference because we discovered that there was no way we could arrange the bedroom furniture so that we could open the wardrobe door if we retained the bed. In a way we were not surprised because everything about the move had been a disaster. This was due mainly to the fact that we had planned it in detail. We had had a small studio built on, bunks fitted for our young son David and infant daughter Penelope (who had joined us shortly after the pianola left) and we had decided to install wall-to-wall carpeting. For economy reasons we also decided that I should fit the carpets myself. The garage was already completed, in spite of a month's delay while the local electricity authority debated whether it was possible to move their pole two feet to the left, and all that was needed was a concrete pad over the mudhole which had developed between the garage and the front door. The builders swore regular oaths that the concrete would be laid before we moved in and that all services would be connected to our total satisfaction.

There was almost a week to go when I started laying our Peacock Blue, Old Gold and Cantaloup carpets and although the morning I had set aside for the job somehow got extended to two days, I think I did a fairly good job. I admit that the pile on those carpets was not very deep but I did not realise that kneeling on them for two days would put me on my back for almost a week. Housemaid's knee is one of those afflictions, like tennis elbow and athlete's foot, which is wide open to ridicule. It matters not how much agony one is suffering; when sympathisers arrive to enquire as to one's health and learn that one has housemaid's

knee they one and all break into shrieks of manic laughter and take their grapes home again. I still have to bite my lip hard to prevent myself from laughing at tennis elbows or athlete's feet but I promise anyone who has never had them that housemaid's knees are not funny.

By the time moving day arrived I could hardly struggle into the car, much less drive it. The day dawned – if that is the right word for it – as a vague lightening of the iron-grey curtain of rain. To make things worse the removal man with whom arrangements had been made had warned us not to pack things. 'Don't pack anything,' he said, 'otherwise we cannot accept responsibility for breakages.' So we didn't and when the pantechnicon arrived the men had no packing cases with them. There was no point in it, they said, since the boss had told them that we had insisted on packing everything ourselves. Everyone knows that you cannot claim to be an artist if you care a tinker's damn what the neighbours think when they sit in their windows watching everything you possess – however intimate – being carried out through the pouring rain under the arms of three saturated and disgruntled men. All I know is that the pains shot up from my knees and attacked my stomach. I was desperately looking round for somewhere to lie down without being trampled by hob-nailed boots.

Our new abode was a modest enough bungalow in a pretty country lane some way out of town. There was a nice piece of garden surrounded by a field where horses grazed. The path from the gate was much longer than the one we were leaving and the lane itself was very narrow. Indeed, when we arrived in the wake of the removal van we discovered that the lane was too narrow to allow the van to turn into the front gate. It was still pouring with rain and the men were dragging our possessions up the path to the front door where there was a bottle-neck. The trouble was that the cement pad between the garage and the front door had only been laid the previous day and had not set, so that the builders, who were still working inside, had placed a plank on bricks across the area. The removal men – wet through to the skin – were trying to carry arms full of linen, chairs, tables and wardrobes across this narrow plank which was whipping up and down like a trampoline. As soon as we arrived we could see that there was already bad blood between the two groups of artisans.

It's true that the front door was a bit narrow and the hall was really a passage of similar width with a right-angle bend in the middle; but the seat of the trouble was the ladder in the middle of this passage, up which one of the builders had ascended into the roof space. Words were being exchanged between the two men who were trying to get the dressing-table past the ladder and the man in the loft. There was a frightening blue flame roaring from the spout of a blow-lamp which was balanced precariously on the very edge of the trap-door opening and it was obviously fear of this falling onto them which was preventing the men below from taking the ladder by storm. I had laid newspapers over the beautiful carpets that had caused my agony to protect them from any soil which might enter on the boots of the removal men, but sheets of newspaper stick to wet boots (I had not allowed for that) and people were tramping hither and thither with pieces of wet paper stuck to their feet, so that they began to look like a parade of shire horses. The pain in my knees had now reached my head and I lay down in the middle of the lounge amid a pile of dirty newspapers and tried to pretend that I was having a nightmare. Men kept coming in with domestic items and saying, 'Where do you want this, Mac?' 'In the studio,' I kept muttering – whatever the object was. All my planning strategy was in tatters like the newspapers. Most of our possessions ended up 'in the studio' crammed, pushed and piled in so tightly that it took us two days to find the kettle.

Rhona was the only person in the milling crowd who had any idea why I was lying in the middle of the floor with my eyes closed. The children thought I was trying to get ideas for *Punch*; God knows what the removal men thought.

'Hello there!' said a voice, 'you'll be Mr Thelwell.' A pleasant-looking gentleman in a homburg hat and smart city suit was smiling down at me. His cheerful wife was peering over his shoulder. 'We're your neighbours from the cottage opposite. We just thought we'd pop in and welcome you to your new home,' he said. 'Don't get up,' he added, leaning over and shaking me warmly by the hand. 'Moving house can be an exhausting business.' They departed with our children who they entertained for the rest of the day.

Rhona finally managed to persuade a removal man to put up a bed. My knees had swollen to such a size that I could hardly get my trousers off and we had not the slightest idea where our night clothes were. I was struggling onto the bed, therefore, in a highly embarrassing state of undress when our solicitor put his head round the bedroom door and asked if I would mind signing some papers.

I gave up planning things after that and it was probably a good thing. After all, look what the planners have done to our towns and cities.

Although I never had any illusions about being a good teacher of art I certainly enjoyed a great deal of the time when I was involved with the students at Wolverhampton. For one thing, although I was officially there to teach design and illustration, the curriculum was pleasantly flexible and I found myself in charge of life-drawing, character-drawing and outdoor painting from time to time. I loved working out of doors and still do. Sometimes when I was a student myself I was the only one to turn up at the appointed site if the weather was bad and I find that painting in the rain can be great fun, particularly if there is no lightning and you can get under a tree. A good downpour can sometimes improve a water-colour out of all recognition.

I had a dilapidated old Standard 8 car at Wolverhampton and I made sure that the students did some outdoor work by picking them up at the college and providing them with free transport into the surrounding countryside. There were usually only about eight or nine boys and girls at a time and although the car was officially a four-seater, it had running boards and a sun-roof. The only thing the sun-roof let in was rain but it was very useful when transporting art students. They didn't mind being crowded – after all they spent their rag-days seeing how many of them could get into a telephone box at one time. They were quite happy being three-deep in the back seat and if there were any over they stood on the running boards with their arms through the sun-roof – all safe and tidy.

We often followed the Albrighton Hunt when there was a meet. I was anxious to get the students to use their sketchbooks as much as possible and the hurly-burly rush and bustle of a hunt was just the thing to make them draw quickly and loosen up their technique. I'm astonished to remember how free and easy the roads were in those days. If riders came sweeping by I would jam on the brakes and the doors would fly open and students would fly out like pigeons from a wicker basket. I was as keen as they were to get some quick notes and sketches and the car would be abandoned with doors wide open in the middle of the lane. When we returned it would be just as we had left it; the engine still running and the doors rising and falling to the steady rhythm of the puffs of blue smoke from the exhaust. We would all pile in again, use a bit of field-craft and try to ambush the hunt at some other likely spot.

Canal near Wolverhampton. Oil on hardboard 32″ × 22″. Painted much later from sketches made near Atherley Junction where I frequently took students for outdoor painting classes.

One day I found myself alone in a woodland clearing. The hunt field and the students with them had gone away with the sounds of the hunt. Suddenly I saw what I thought at first was a small grey dog coming straight towards me. The little creature did not seem to notice me and as it drew nearer I realised that it was a mud-spattered, exhausted little fox. He suddenly became aware of me and turned aside towards a moss-covered dry wall, which he made several ineffectual attempts to jump over. He seemed totally spent and, on a sudden impulse, I ran forward, grasped him by his grimy coat and bundled him onto the top of the wall. He dropped over the other side and I never saw him again. I stood quite still listening and had just realised from the hound music that the pack was heading back in my direction when an alarming thought struck me: I probably reeked of fox. I ran the quarter-mile back to the car in commendable time, fell inside and slammed the doors. I sat there, mud-spattered and with my tongue lolling and fervently hoping that the scruffy little fox had also made it to a safe bolt hole.

For the uninitiated, character-drawing means drawing people with their clothes on and life-drawing means drawing people with their clothes off. At least, that's what they meant when I was in art schools. They are both honourable and useful occupations for artists, and people who sit or pose for them are, in my experience, as honourable and hardworking as the average vicar. I mention this only because there are a lot of people about who are not artists and who have the idea that those who are must by definition be a bit odd.

Taking Cover. (*From* Sporting Prints.)

The Mirror. Water-colour and body colour on tinted paper.

Let's not beat about the bush: it is this business about drawing people in the nude that gets them all steamed up. If there are any nervous parents about, let me reassure them. You are quite safe in letting young Nigel go to the art school and draw nude ladies. I can promise you that after the first ten minutes his hands will stop shaking and he will be as keen on producing beautiful drawings to show you as you would be yourself – keener probably. Furthermore, he will be as free from embarrassment as the lady herself – and it might even cure his stammer.

The only embarrassing incident I can recall occurred in the 'life' room at Wolverhampton which was on the top floor and had a large sloping window to admit maximum light. About twenty students were hard at work when the model beckoned me over with her eyes (models are not supposed to move anything else). Her lips hardly moved either as she muttered, 'Look at the tax office roof.' The tax office was about a hundred yards away and four men in overalls were perched along the edge of the roof (four storeys up) leaning forward in such a way that the slightest breeze would have tipped them over the edge. I had a quiet word with a student who hurried down to the yard and shouted at them to go away which they promptly did. Everyone in the district must have heard what he shouted, which is what caused my embarrassment. *I* didn't tell him to call them *that*.

The object of 'character-drawing' is to train the student to observe the particular characteristics of individual people which make them different from all other human beings. It is not just the shape of the head and facial features that are important but the general bearing of the figure, the hands, the feet, the clothes they wear and the way they wear them. It follows, therefore, that it is not a good idea to use the same model too often. Indeed the more models one can call upon the better.

The layman may well imagine that as character models are not required to remove even their hats, the drawing master has a much easier time than when he is handling life models, if you follow my meaning. And that is where the layman can be

wrong. The trouble is that being an artist's model is a difficult and exacting profession and there are not too many of them about. Consequently one has to fall back, as it were, on amateurs who are far less reliable. Quite apart from the fact that the average person, of whatever age, finds it difficult to sit still for more than ten seconds at a time, casual models tend to regard the whole business as a bit of a joke and don't bother to turn up or take fright and chicken out at the last minute. When you have a class of eager students sitting by their easels with pencils poised and tongues at the corner of their mouths this can be a problem. It was frequently necessary for me to ask my students to talk quietly among themselves whilst I went out into the street and tried to entice people in to sit for them. This can not only be a difficult and embarrassing operation but it can be positively dangerous.

Older people tend to be rather better models for character-drawing because long experience of life has usually left its effect upon their faces and they are thus more interesting to draw. Luckily there was often a fair sprinkling of senior citizens taking their ease on the seats in the public garden outside the college and I got to know one or two of them who were glad enough to earn a few shillings by dozing indoors. If they were not about, however, things could get difficult.

On one of these forays among the flower-beds I spotted a sweet old lady sitting on a seat and plucking at a knitted glove which was disintegrating to the point where all her finger ends were fully exposed to the sunshine. She had pale delicate skin which was textured with fine lines, like a Ming vase, and bright, alert little eyes. Her hair was like a handful of yellow straw which stuck out in random spikes from beneath a black velvet hat with faded flowers on it. She was a beautiful character. I was glad to see that there was no one else on the seat and I sat down myself and wished her good afternoon. She looked at me in a quizzical way.

'Pardon me, madam,' I said, 'I am an art teacher at the college over there and the model we engaged has let us down. The students have no one to sit for them and I wondered . . .'

'He-he-he!' she shrieked in a voice like a train whistle. 'He-he-he! What! *Me* deary, at my time of life?' It was a warm, sunny afternoon and the gardens were full of people taking their ease. Every one of them turned round and every face registered shock, horror and outrage. I thought it better not to run and tried to reason with her.

'Please madam!' I said, 'don't misunderstand. You would only have to sit on a chair for a little while and we pay a small fee.'

'He-he-he,' she hooted. 'Want me in the rude do you, deary?'

She was still shrieking when I disappeared through the college door and up the stairs to the waiting students. They were all draped about the room banging the walls and stamping their feet on the floor in helpless laughter. The windows which were open overlooked the gardens and the whole class had been watching. We settled, as we had done more than once before, for one of the students volunteering to sit for the rest of the group. Vera was a good sport.

'Want me in the rude, deary?' she grinned, as she took up her pose on the chair.

From *Punch* and *Thelwell Country*.

*Rodeo. One of a series of colour cartoons
produced as posters, greetings cards and jigsaw puzzles.*

6: PONIES WITH *PUNCH*

I had been teaching for about two years before I summoned up enough courage to submit work to *Punch*. I told myself that I had enough freelance work to do already but the truth was that I was afraid of rejection. In the early fifties there was a great vogue for cartoons of the non-art type and a widespread belief that a humorous drawing is always improved by the exclusion of any detail or stroke of the pen which is not intrinsic to the joke. This approach was noticeable not only in Britain but on the continent and in America also and I was well aware of the excellence of some of the work produced in this manner. I greatly admired the work of Saul Steinberg in *The New Yorker* and the delicious naïve drawings of James Thurber and André François, but my own work had little in common with the type of drawing which was prevalent and popular at the time.

I sold a small drawing to *Punch* in 1952 and was rather shaken when a friend of mine, who was a sensitive artist and a fine painter with a love also of humorous art, told me that I should be ashamed of myself for producing a drawing which was, as he put it, 'pandering to the non-art crowd'. What was the use of good draughtsmanship, he asked me, if I was prepared to do indifferent work for money? It was a shattering little lecture but I knew that he was right and I have been grateful for his reprimand ever since. That weekend I made a drawing of a gypsy encampment simply because I wanted to play about with the detail and enjoy the work. I decided on the caption when the picture was almost finished – which is quite the wrong way to produce cartoons or humorous drawings. *Punch* bought it as a half-page and paid me 10 guineas for it and it was the beginning of a 25-year-long association with that famous magazine during which I made over 1,500 drawings for it including 60 front covers.

'It's their simplicity that I envy.'

This is the first large cartoon published by Punch in 1952. I made the drawing first and worked out the caption later, which is quite the wrong way to go about producing cartoons.

(above right) This was a comment on the lunacy of putting picture windows into housing estates where the only view was through the picture window into the house opposite. From Punch, 1970.

(below right) This was a tilt at the weakness of design of high-rise housing units at the time of the Ronan Point disaster. From Punch, 1971.

'You'd better get washed and dressed. They're having company.'

'Door!'

MOTOR NUMBER

This Week :
The Charge of the Heavy Brigade

18—24 APRIL 1973 15p WEEKLY

A DAY AT THE RACES

4—10 AUGUST 1976 25p WEEKLY

This week :
So you think you'd like to be a farmer ?

Punch cover designs based on the
main theme of the particular issues.

As for so many cartoonists over its long history, *Punch* was the nucleus of and predominant influence on my career and I devoted more time to it than to any other publication. Working regularly for *Punch* not only gave me a sense of kudos and achievement but brought me into personal contact with the top humorous artists of the time and my drawings to a world-wide public. It also encouraged me to explore the humour of the British countryside which has always been the main interest of my life.

In his introduction to my first book *Angels on Horseback*, published in 1957, J. B. Boothroyd wrote: 'In mid-Victorian times it was difficult to open a copy [of *Punch*] without being trampled.' He was right, of course, and there was plenty of rich country humour in it right up until the Second World War. After the war it seemed to evaporate, as if the countryside had ceased to exist, but I cannot claim that I noticed this and moved

into a hole in the market. On the contrary, I drew country subjects because I wanted to and it was some time before I noticed that I was more or less the only cartoonist doing so regularly. I expected others to appear at any time but strangely they did not, nor have they in more than thirty years. At least I cannot name one.

It was while we were living in Codsall, in August 1956, that I was offered a job as cartoonist on that excellent daily newspaper, the *News Chronicle*, sadly no longer with us. Although I was required to produce only two cartoons per week the job made it impossible to continue teaching at the College of Art and I decided to take the final plunge and become entirely freelance. There was a small hiccup at the beginning, because after working for one very full day in the *News Chronicle* office I realised that I could not work in the noisy, bustling atmosphere in which journalists seem to thrive, so I returned home the same night and composed a

'Hey Pete! There's a real beauty over here
with vital statistics of two and a half, nothing and ninety-six.'

Line and Zipatone cartoon for *News Chronicle*, 1958.

letter to the editor thanking him for offering me the job but explaining that I did not think I could produce my best work in a newspaper office. To my delight he wrote back by return post saying in effect 'OK, work from home', which I did for the rest of my time with the paper.

Working to a 'deadline' for a daily newspaper is a well paid but exacting occupation and I am full of admiration for the many great cartoonists who have continued to amuse and entertain the public for so many years. The main problem, as I saw it, was that not only must an idea be produced for each occasion but the idea had to come within a strictly limited time in order to allow one to complete the drawing the same day and get it onto a London train for collection in time to be published the next morning. It could be nerve-wracking if one thought about it too deeply. Supposing an idea just will not materialise tomorrow . . . ? Supposing I mess up the drawing and have to start again . . . ? Supposing I get run down on the way to the station and miss the train . . . ? Supposing the train is held up by train robbers and they mistake the package for valuables . . . ? Supposing it gets there safe and sound and the editor hates it . . . ?

Working for magazines is less worrying because the deadline is usually much less pressing and there is more time for editors to substitute other material if something goes wrong. I did a number of jobs years ago for the American magazine *Esquire.* The artwork had to go by air – 'Oh please God don't let the plane be hijacked to Cuba.'

The thing is not to get neurotic about it – even when the art editor of *Punch* buys you a pint in the Savage Club bar and then tells you he's got bad news for you.

'Remember the cover you did for us of Mr Punch holding Toby high above his head so that the dog could watch the dog show on the other side of the fence? Right! Well, we've lost it! . . . Drink up, Norman. You'll be all right in a minute. It won't affect your pay . . . Well it's a bit complicated really. You see there was this new lad whose job it was to take things from the office to the printing works. It seems that a girl at the works was getting married and there was a whip-round in the office to contribute to a wedding present. The money was put into an envelope and he was told to deliver the cover design to the printers and the money to the lady who was organising the wedding present. They rang from the works in the afternoon to ask why the cover had not arrived. Time was pressing. It had been sent that morning along with the wedding present money. What wedding present money? Haven't you had it? Not as far as I know, who brought it? Arnold. Arnold hasn't been here. He needs someone's boot behind him, that lad. We've got his home address. We'll get someone round there to have a word with his mother. We're waiting for that cover . . . It was the next day before the story broke. His mother hadn't seen Arnold all day so they asked if they could wait and it was nearly six o'clock before he wandered in. Well, he was on the way to the works when he met this girl he knew and they went to the pictures with the wedding present money. Yes! yes! What did he do with the cover? Well he couldn't take this girl to the pictures and hold onto the package so he threw it over the wall onto a rubbish dump. Find it? You must be joking! They dump about ten tons of rubbish per hour on that tip . . . So do you think you could do it again, Norman? We'll have to have it by Friday.'

I did, and they paid me for both pieces of work; but I would dearly like to have been the one to put my boot behind Arnold.

Some time in 1953 *Punch* published a cartoon of mine which involved a blacksmith and a child on a pony. As far as I was concerned it was just another idea based on the kind of countryside subjects I enjoyed drawing. There was a noticeable increase in letters from readers about that cartoon and I am surprised to find that it was almost a year later before I did another drawing which involved a child on a pony. This cartoon also brought in a lot of letters and, although for every pony drawing I did for *Punch* I did at least fifty on other subjects, the pony theme took on an instant popularity

' 'ow do *they* feel then?'

This is the first drawing I ever made of a child on a pony.
It was published in Punch *in 1953 and it was almost a year*
before I did another pony and child cartoon.

which astonished me. I had done drawings of horses since childhood and had learned the general anatomy of humans and horses from library books pretty thoroughly by the time I was fifteen, but I loved drawing cows and pigs and chickens too and my liking for horses sprang from the fact that they are beautiful to draw – like ships and trees.

I suspect that there was another underlying reason why I enjoyed drawing them, however. They are nervous, unpredictable creatures, likely to take off in a shower of flying turf and thunder at the drop of a riding hat and they symbolise for me the nervous insecurity of almost all living creatures including humans. I have always admired the relatively few calm, self-assured people I have known in my life but most human beings find life a bit of a problem and are pretty jumpy under the skin. It is this insecurity when dealing with other people or with animals or even with inanimate objects that I find both comical and endearing in human beings and in animals too.

'You're *bound* to feel nervous the first time on television.'

When drawing for a weekly magazine like Punch it is not possible, or even desirable, for ideas to be as hotly topical as those in a daily newspaper must be. It is, however, most important for a cartoonist to watch carefully for ways in which the world is changing and comment upon them. The use of films of surgical operations as evening 'entertainment' on television and the widespread use of chemical fertilisers to increase farm crops were two such developments.

'They could have done with a bit more sulphate of ammonia.'

My own encounters with horses as a means of transport had been few and mercifully far between but after the last war when mechanisation more or less took over from working horses in both town and country a new phenomenon appeared. Riding horses for pleasure ceased to be the exclusive pastime of the monied classes and children who would previously have driven their parents demented trying to wheedle a bicycle out of them – or even a doll's pram – now demanded a horse of their own. 'Oh can I, Mummy? Oh can I, Daddy? Why not?' Stamp, stamp. 'I'm the only girl in my whole class at school who doesn't have a pony.' Furthermore, you no longer needed social standing to join pony clubs and win rosettes and things by charging through timber barricades like they did almost nightly on television. A child who had no pony could lose face among her peers and go to the bad. Parents who took the plunge, of course, began to worry not about where the next meal was coming from to feed their children but where the next ton of pony nuts or hay was coming from to feed the pony in the garden shed. The feminist movement was sweeping over us all like the Krakatoa tidal wave and girls had to keep their end up, so to speak. Rivalry became keen. 'Who does Georgina Fetlock-Jones think she is? I've broken my collar bone as many times as she has.'

There were a couple of ponies grazing in the paddock which surrounded our Codsall garden. They were small and round and fat and of very uncertain temper. Not that I ever went too near them, but I could see them rolling their eyes and flaring their great nostrils from my studio desk. They were owned by two little girls about three feet high who could have done with losing a few ounces themselves. They would arrive to collect their mounts in yellow pullovers, tiny jodhpurs and velvet safety helmets. I could hear the air whistle as they tested out their whips – so could Thunder and Lightning, who pointedly ignored them and went on grazing. You could tell they were watching the situation, however, because their ears disappeared under their shaggy manes as they laid them back.

As the children got near the ponies would swing round and present their ample hindquarters and give a few lightning kicks which the children would side-step as calmly as if they were avoiding the kitchen table, and they had the head collars on those animals before they knew what was happening. I was astonished at how meekly they were led away; but they were planning vengeance – you could tell by their eyes.

One morning I heard the sounds of battle among the dandelions and saw the most amazing sight. The two little equestrians were locked in mortal combat. I'd seen plenty of children fighting before (I once watched a spectacular punch-up on roller-skates in an asphalt playground) but nothing like this. I'd seen pictures of jousts in books and one or two in films but never a real live combat on caparisoned mounts. It's true that they had neither battle-axes, shields nor spiked metal balls on chains, but the whips were making livid lines on the velvet hats and they were manoeuvring their ponies with a skill which would have made King Arthur's boys green with envy. It was a bit of an anticlimax when their mother appeared: tears and shouts of 'She started it', 'No I didn't', 'Did,' 'Didn't', 'Did', 'Didn't' and they were led away, still mounted.

The ponies didn't seem much concerned but I couldn't help wondering if they'd planned the whole thing in the field there the night before. 'Hey Thunder, I've got a great idea! Let's keep bumping them into each other in the morning. See how much they can take before they lose their tempers.' 'I like it, Lightning – I like it!'

Incidents like that are rarely translatable into humorous drawings just as they happened. They are the material from which cartoons may be made rather than the finished product. Each component needs to be extracted, analysed and modified if necessary and reassembled (often in several different ways) until something worthwhile begins to emerge. The incident had great potential. It was visually comical and exciting and full of the fast movement which I like. It was an unusual sight in itself but was basically just a variation on the old

'Come along girls! Playtime's over.'

familiar kids' squabble which everyone has seen a
hundred times. This familiarity was also a great
advantage because humans laugh more readily at
things they understand and feel comfortable with.

The reality, however, was that the whole affair
petered out like a damp squib when mother arrived
and the components needed a catalyst to make
them gel and some kind of twist or spark to make
them explode. Most children's fights which ended

in physical contact I associated with playtime at
school, so it seemed a good idea to set the scene
in a riding school and give the teacher a bowler
hat to go with the school bell. Then what about a
twist in the tail? Well, if the battle looks alarming
enough and 'teacher' treats the whole thing as
normal it might work. At that point all one can do
is draw the thing up, and hope it does. Sometimes
it does, sometimes not.

Rhona and me with Penny and David at Codsall, 1956.

I used to cut out my own drawings when they were reproduced in magazines, with the idea of pasting them into some sort of folio which could be useful to show to agents, editors and anyone else who might offer me work. I imagine that most aspiring artists do the same and I did make a start with the paste-brush but, happily, the cuttings began to gather rather quickly and I could rarely find the time to mount them up. The consequence was that they began to get dog-eared or lost. It was this state of affairs which made me think that it would be very useful if I could put them together in some sort of printed book. It would look more impressive and professional to prospective clients too, so I asked the advice of an artists' agent who was dealing with some of my work.

'Don't waste your time, my boy,' he said. 'Books of humorous drawings are a drug on the market' (it was the first time I had heard that expression). 'People pick them up in bookshops, thumb through them and put them down.'

I was a bit disappointed but it sounded good advice and I dropped the idea.

It was only a few weeks later, however, when I was discussing designing some dust-jackets with Frank Herrmann, the production manager of Methuen, that he asked me if I had ever thought of doing a book.

'Well, now you come to mention it,' I said, 'it has crossed my mind, but my agent says it would be a drug on the market.'

I felt like Gracie Fields when she took her harp to a party but nobody asked her to play. Frank Herrmann didn't agree with the agent's views on the matter and said he would like to see what ideas I had. It was Alan Delgado, who later became my agent and close friend for many years, who suggested that I should keep the book to a single theme and the theme should be horses, with particular emphasis on children's riding. What good advice that turned out to be. *Angels on Horseback* was published in 1957 and has never been out of print since. But the gentleman who told me about drugs on the market took the whole affair in very good part: whenever I saw him he would go into a comical charade of shooting himself.

Angels on Horseback in various editions since publication.

From *Thelwell Country*.

'It'll be the most disastrous year
I've ever known if this lot catches fire.'

From *Top Dog*.

FIRST PRINCIPLES

From *Riding Academy*.

'No! No! Deirdre,
you've got the wrong foot in that stirrup.'

*'Penelope' first appeared
in the* Sunday Express.
*These strip cartoons
were later published
in book form by Methuen.*

THE FIRESIDE JUNGLE

From *Up the Garden Path.*

Indoor plants can do much to improve
the visual appearance of your rooms.

Others are drawn by
its exciting uncertainties.   From *The Complete Tangler.*

One of the small illustration jobs which I did during the teaching years was for the *Birmingham Post*. On Saturday mornings they published a small feature on subjects which were designed to appeal to a minority readership. One series was on angling, which no doubt was of great interest to many readers judging by the fact that anglers and particularly publishers of angling books have claimed it to be the biggest participation sport in Britain; another series was on 'Keeping Hens for Pleasure and Profit' and another on wine. The editor's idea was to include a small illustration with a touch of humour about it which would help with the layout and draw the eye of readers to the written matter.

The articles were not written in a humorous manner – indeed their chief object was to impart useful information on the subject – and I found it difficult to produce a cartoon on the theme every week. What I did notice was that almost all information imparted by experts tends by its very nature to become rather pompous and I decided to seize on this fact and illustrate certain lines in the text as if I had misunderstood their meaning. Thus, the statement 'Allow two square feet per bird' was illustrated by a man painting neat squares on the chicken-house floor whilst his hens sat disconsolately in their allotted space. Following this principle one can imagine how simple it was to illustrate such statements as: 'On the topic of wine glasses . . . the rule is simply to use whatever is available' or 'Another aspect of wine is the wonderful argumentative possibilities it possesses' or 'Ensure that your birds' feet are dry before they enter the pophole'. It was a method of extracting humour from otherwise serious or pedantic instructions and information which led to a number of books in later years.

Talk to them . . . they enjoy a friendly word.

Do not let them flap around
by holding them only by their legs.

From *Birmingham Post*, 1956.

7: THE SOUTH COUNTRY

Chalk Pits in the Test Valley, 18 July 1976. Water-colour 10″ × 14″.

When I took on regular work for *The News Chronicle* as well as for *Punch* and casual contributions to other magazines, pamphlets, book-jackets and illustrations, and occasional advertising work, I could no longer find the time to go on teaching and I became full-time freelance in the summer of 1956. This freed us from the necessity of living near my work and, indeed, it made it possible for us to live more or less anywhere we wished, provided that reasonable contact could be kept with publications I was working for; and Rhona and I spent the next three years looking around Britain for what we considered to be an ideal spot. The country lane in Codsall was already beginning to attract the developers and within a few years it became swamped with residential estates so that it quickly lost the charm it had had.

Finding the ideal spot, however, is not as easy as it sounds. When one has to work each day at a particular location the task is at least reduced to finding the best place to live within an area convenient to the place of work. Suddenly we had no such restriction and even in these small islands the field was vast. The alarming boom in property values was still a long way off and Britain was littered with buildings for sale.

Now it happened that Frank Herrmann, who had first suggested that I should produce a book, was also scouring the country for an ideal place to live and we discovered that we were both receiving masses of estate agents' particulars through our doors with almost every post.

'Why don't you do a book based on the flowery phrases which estate agents use in their literature?' he suggested.

It seemed an excellent idea. Frank sent me a parcel of his own collection of blurb to add to my own, so I had plenty of material to work on. It was not difficult to find suitable phrases to illustrate; one only had to sift through the piles of sales details and there they were. 'Ripe for modernisation'; 'Ready to walk into'; 'In the heart of the Puckeridge Hunt'; 'A unique property'; 'In a quiet backwater'; 'With direct frontage to the river'; etc. The material was so rich that there was

a danger of going too far with it. So I restricted it to one chapter and devoted other sections to the agents themselves, to surveyors and their reports, to buyers and sellers and so on.

By chance there was a strike (of printers, I think) at *Punch* which released me from the urgency of finding ideas. The strike lasted only two weeks but it was enough. *A Place of Your Own* was completed from cover to cover in that time – by far the fastest book I ever produced, such was the abundance of material. It led ten years later to a larger volume on the same theme called *This Desirable Plot – A Dream-House Hunter's Nightmare* which also dealt with weekend cottages and the popular pastime of converting redundant railway stations, pubs, barns, mills, forges, village schools, etc., into 'character' residences. I was delighted to find that these books were very popular with estate agents as well as the general public.

This property affords
fascinating possibilities.

From *This Desirable Plot.*

To quote from *A Place of Your Own*:

When freed some time ago from the necessity of living near my work, my wife and I gave a whoop of joy, threw a few things into a suitcase, left the children with our parents and set off to find our dream house. That was three years and eight months ago to be precise and the process has been repeated in exactly the same way so often since that we don't care to think about it. In exactly the same way, that is, except for the whoop of joy. We have pushed our heads into airing cupboards from Shrewsbury to Winchester and scrambled into attics from Bishops Teignton to Brighton. We have inspected houses so dreadfully empty that the sound of a twig scratching on the window has sent us flying into each other's arms and smiled and nodded our way through cottages so overcrowded that we couldn't get into the hall until the dog was pushed into the backyard. We have come to understand the most flowery phrases employed by estate agents and to shudder at the hollow laugh of probing surveyors.

We tread as warily as cats on the most solid-looking floors and listen attentively to every piece of wood more than five years old. We have learned that looking for a dream house is a long-drawn-out nightmare and that leaving your Airedale with friends is the quickest way to lose them.

You won't be warned, of course, but at least I've tried.

Although we covered a wide sweep of Britain we found ourselves constantly returning to South Hampshire around the area where I was billeted with the 2nd East Yorkshire Regiment in 1942. I remembered how beautiful the countryside was and how impressed I had been by the great trees and delightful villages we passed through on our way to Hursley Park – even through pouring rain in columns of three with full packs on our backs, sweating and tired beneath our dripping gas capes. Hursley Park camp in 1942 was one of the worst collections of tatty Nissen huts and rat-infested quarters that we ever occupied. In such circumstances it says a great deal for Hampshire that I found the whole area around Romsey, Winchester and the New Forest altogether enchanting.

One of the exercises we did at that time was concerned with crossing rivers by means of kapok floats which were strung out like animated stepping stones. They were simply anchored on each side of the river by ropes which did nothing to prevent each float from swinging, dipping and lurching about in the current. The idea was to form up in a column facing the contraption and when the sergeant shouted 'Go, go, go!' we went – leaping like lunatics from one slippery, dancing black cushion to the next. I think one or two men actually got across without the water reaching higher than their trouser tops but by the time two or three pairs of army boots had hit them the floats were bouncing up in the air and landing end on – some of them turning over. Almost everyone went in, backwards, sideways or head first. I swear that the scene would have made the Keystone Cops look like a church outing. The only light relief for us was when the sergeant fell between two floats and got his legs tangled in the ropes.

Little did I realise as we sat on the bank, emptying water out of our boots, that our underpants and socks were saturated with some of the most valuable water in the world. For this was the River Test, possibly the most exclusive, expensive dry-fly trout fishing in the world; and even less did I realise that one day I would live on its banks, stalk its fat trout and wander back to our cottage on balmy summer evenings with a wellington full of my own trout water. How I wish I could remember now just where, along these flower-decked banks, we all came near to drowning in it.

We finally bought an old house in the Hampshire village of Braishfield which had been for sale for several years without attracting a

*The Sluice Gate at Tumbling Bay
on the River Test.* Water-colour 12″ × 8″.

Willows in the Water Meadows, Hampshire.
Water-colour 16″ × 20″.

Church View, Braishfield,
as it looked when we first bought it.

The proportions of the building were good, however, and I took some photographs of it and did some retouching. I painted out the narrow, nightmare, brick porch and painted in a wider one of better proportion with a curving Georgian-type lead roof. With the paint-brush I opened up a bricked-up bedroom window, added white shutters to the façade and replaced the grey untidy slates with darker tiles. I had always been interested in rural buildings as well as church architecture and I really enjoyed converting the house to fit the retouched photographs. I quickly discovered that the average builder (and who can blame him?) seems to take more personal interest in his job if he has seen an accurate picture of what he is aiming at.

In spite of the fact that the house had not found a buyer for so long I was surprised that, once the front elevation looked like the retouched photograph, several people came to enquire whether it was still for sale, even though we had at that time done nothing to modernise or refurbish the inside apart from decorating.

purchaser. It was, at first sight, an ugly house in a beautiful overgrown and neglected setting. It stood on a hillside above a steeply sloping orchard with four ancient apple trees, shaggy with peeling bark and mistletoe. They grew in a mature bog amid great tussocks of reeds and giant docks. Above the orchard the ground rose in three levels round the house to a sizeable garden behind. An old yew tree shaded this high plateau, and a quince tree lay in a sweeping curve along the ground and up into a burst of pale green foliage against the dark yew. Birds bustled in the high neglected hedges which enclosed the garden and through a gap cows grazed on the sunlit farmland which swept away to thickly wooded distance.

Change of address card.

106

It took much longer to deal with the two acres of tumbledown outhouses and rampant jungle which surrounded them. To the right of the old garden behind a stand of conifers was a large yard with a red brick barn, a cowshed, chicken-houses and an old Nissen hut covered with ivy, in which it was impossible to cough without bringing down a shower of rust from the roof. Was it, I wondered, the one I had slept in only a mile or two away at Hursley Camp seventeen years before, sold as army surplus and destined to go on haunting me? It could well have been, judging by its parlous state. The front of the house overlooked the village church which peeped through great plumes of foliage and beyond the glittering weather-cock rooks circled like burnt paper above tall dark pines. The roofs of cottages lay below among the trees and the undulating Hampshire countryside rolled away to the horizon.

Cherry Hill: the same house as it appeared a year or two later.

David and Penny had acquired a black-and-white border collie pup from a litter in the village whom we called Bess. She not only joined in all games but took a keen interest in our work too. It seemed a good idea to plant a few things as early as possible so that they would have time to settle down while we were slashing our way through the rest of the jungle. I wanted some Virginia creeper on the house, so, as soon as we had cleared a few square feet of ground near the wall, I planted a couple of pieces which I bought from the local garden centre. Bess watched the operation with interest. Later in the day Bess appeared at the kitchen door with Virginia creeper hanging from each side of her mouth. I tried all the tricks the dog-training manuals recommend but she just stared back at me through her ridiculous green moustache. The only thing left was to make a grab at her, which I did. She streaked off into the jungle and I never saw that Virginia creeper again.

The only practical means of progress over most of our property was slow, determined chopping. We chopped for weeks into brushwood and saplings, weeds, chicken wire, reeds, docks and ivy and, on one memorable morning, into a wasp's nest. There are some traumas in one's life that one cannot talk about. Suffice it to say that I finally outran the incensed wasps and when I staggered into the house and Rhona had satisfied herself that I had not had a heart attack, she produced a 'dolly blue' bag and started painting the stings. It took her ages to locate and deal with them all (wasps have no sense of modesty) and by the time she had finished I looked like an ancient Briton who had dragged himself back home after being beaten up on the battlefield. The wasp incident tended to slow down my clearing operations. After all, there could have been another lot waiting for me at every swing of the machete. In fact it was two weeks before I came across an old farm cart which was settling into a mouldering heap in the middle of the paddock. We enjoyed bonfires of a size and extravagance greater than we had seen before and uncovered a succession of fascinating relics of past occupation, from old rings and broken clay pipes to rusty baths and rotting harness.

A neighbour's child, playing with our children on the orchard slope, fell into a water hole up to his waist and was lucky not to have gone into a deeper one. We had an anxious time there, too, when a heavy tractor bogged down axle deep while

Desert horsemen.
Water-colour and body colour on tinted paper 6″ × 7″.

In the Forest.
Oil on canvas board 23″ × 29″.

trying to pull out another tractor which was even deeper in the morass. At last we managed to lay a series of land drains down the slope and cover them up. We never noticed any water running from them, but it gave us a feeling that we were getting somewhere. The hedge was pulled out from the top of the orchard and by a process of sheer persistence a drive was built across the unstable ground to the lane below. On either side of this the ground settled into a comparatively solid, pudding-like consistency with a more or less even surface; and in time we were able to enjoy a lush lawn in place of the intractable bog. There were a lot of frogs about in those days, however, and they roamed our lawns in dozens. When we started the motor mower up, someone had to go ahead of the machine trying to frighten the frogs. It was a long and frustrating occupation. In retrospect, however, the trouble was well worth it. Frogs now seem to be almost totally extinct in this part of Hampshire and I am surprised to realise that I have seen only one frog in the local water meadows in the past ten years or more. If we had not taken the trouble to scare them from the path of our mower in the early sixties we might now be racked with guilty feelings that we were partly responsible for their extinction. Perhaps, like foxes, the frogs have decided to go to town; my brother Alan has a small goldfish bowl in his garden in Liverpool which, at a certain time of the year, is so full of frogs that his goldfish can hardly move.

There was a large heap of mature horse manure against the wall of the chicken-house when we took over, which was covered with nettles. When we finally got around to disturbing the giant weeds we discovered a positive harvest of mushrooms. They grew thick and fast in all sizes and cutting them seemed to provoke them into frenzied production. We were suddenly swamped with mushrooms. They were in the broken-down greenhouse, too, against the walls of the barn and under the rubbish in the Nissen hut. We became nervous of moving things; we knew what we would find underneath. We had read *The Day of the Triffids* and we began to feel jumpy.

Country people believe there is an antidote to everything and in this case it proved to be my brother and his family, who are mushroom gourmets. They came down from Liverpool for a holiday and the mushroom army suffered heavy casualties. Before they left they carried out mopping-up operations and cut every mushroom still above ground, piling them into every crevice in the car – between the luggage, under the seats. We never saw a single mushroom on the place again.

I had hoped to convert the old brick barn into a studio, but the building was split from roof to foundations on both sides and quite obviously was in a dangerous condition. It was taken down, therefore, for safety's sake; but I used the soft red bricks to build a wall round the old garden at the top of the hill and I built a studio there from cedarwood. It was a lovely place to work at all seasons of the year.

Thinking of funny ideas is a very serious business and I am amazed at how many people imagine that life in the house of a cartoonist is a laugh a minute for him and for his family. This is not only a false assumption: the reverse is true most of the time. The trouble is that once a cartoon is completed and delivered one is out of work until one gets another successful idea. When we breadwinners are sitting at our desks on a wet Monday morning staring at a blank sheet of paper lit by the grey light filtering through the pouring rain outside we can be quite grumpy. It is not the time for our children to jump on our backs, or for our wives to announce that the washing machine has broken down and soapsuds are creeping up the hall.

Whilst the studio was being built up the garden I worked in the house and, for some time, was irritated by a constant, high-pitched, whining note which made concentration quite impossible. It was the kind of insidious sound which is noticeable only when one is quietly trying to think. I put my ear to every electrical and mechanical gadget in the house and then to every inanimate object without discovering the source of the irritation. Like a dripping tap in the wakeful small hours of the

Pen-and-ink sketches of weeds and wild flowers, from A Plank Bridge by a Pool.

night, it could not be ignored. I became convinced that I would have to locate the cause or go quietly mad. I was staring out of the window at a grey sky broken only by the finely etched lines of the telephone wires when a snatch of verse, learned in the Upper Third form, sprang into my mind:

And ringing shrilly, taut and lithe, within the wind a core of sound,
The wire from Romney town to Hythe alone its airy journey wound.

I rang the G P O. 'Please,' I said, 'send someone quickly; the telephone wires are driving me crazy.' I was surprised at the speed with which two men arrived, and it was some time later that I realised they must have thought I was some sort of latter-day Quasimodo. The three of us stood in the room listening intently and I was relieved to find that they could hear it too. They went outside and slackened the wires and all was peace again.

When we took it over the place was known as Church View. We planted flowering cherry trees by the gate and changed its name to Cherry Hill. It proved a happy place to live and to work, and our children were happy there, too. As we pushed ahead with clearing-up operations we amassed large quantities of wood which was no longer sound enough to be used again and from time to time we had bonfires. Sometimes they were just a family affair, with everyone sitting round them as dusk fell and eating toffee apples, but sometimes we held off until my brother came down with Kath and their children.

The most memorable bonfire took place on the fifth of November in 1960. Our children had quickly made friends in the village – and so had we – and we invited a lively group to the Guy Fawkes party. There was a plentiful supply of sausages on sticks, toffee apples and fizzy lemonade for the children; and it fell to the fathers to deal with the pyrotechnics. I had supplied a generous collection of fireworks, spurred on by the fear of seeming parsimonious if they ran out before the children had had enough. Probably for the

Yew Tree Farm, Coniston. Pencil sketch.

Cornworthy, Devon. Fountain-pen sketch.

113

same reason the other dads did the same. By the time things got under way we had an embarrassment of explosives and it became clear to us fathers that we were all going to be needed to apply matches to blue paper if we were going to get through it all. I admit that I should have organised things better but I had not counted on guests bringing fireworks; I admit also that I should never have dumped them all in the one big cardboard box. It was not all my fault, though. We should have called a meeting and decided who was going to set off what and where from, but we didn't.

I think the first hint of panic swept over me when there were six rockets in the sky at the same time and someone said something about thatched roofs. The mums had hauled their offspring back to a safe distance, however, before a stray whizz-bang landed in the cardboard ammunition dump and all the dads ran for cover, too. It was the Queen's Jubilee before we saw another display like that one.

Thatched Roofs under Repair at King's Sourbourne.
Fountain-pen sketch.

8: HOME AND ABROAD

Griante, Northern Italy. Water-colour 11″ × 8″.

Throughout the sixties I was so involved with freelance work for newspapers, magazines and various periodicals that I had much less time to paint for the pleasure of doing so than I would have liked; and when I look back at my records for those years I am surprised by the volume of work I managed to get through, particularly as I spent a lot of time outdoors working in the garden. By the late summer of 1960 I had produced 387 rather detailed cartoons for the *News Chronicle*; and when I went into the house one evening to watch the television news I was shocked to hear that the *News Chronicle* had gone out of business that very day, apparently without any warning. Certainly I had not heard any hint of impending problems. Even the BBC seemed to have very little information on what had brought about such a

sudden disaster. I went into the newspaper office the next morning to try to find out what was happening, but even there no one seemed to know anything. There was an air of complete bewilderment as if everyone in the entire building was stunned.

I never did find out what had really happened and I believe that many people far more deeply involved with the paper than I was never understood either. I had been employed on annual contracts and had always worked at home after the first day in the office, so that it was far less of a disaster for me than it was for very many others. Nevertheless, it meant a sudden and unexpected drop in income for me, too, and I was very glad that I had never become totally involved with any single publication.

It is surprising how little the world changes in these changing times. I had a cartoon in that final issue of the *News Chronicle*. It showed the inside of a sign-writing workshop with men hard at work and stacks of posters everywhere. Each pile had a message: 'Down with traffic wardens', 'No blood sports', 'No bases here – Yanks go home', 'Unilateral disarmament', 'Abolish the eleven plus', 'What about the pensioners?', etc. The boss was looking pleased with his booming business and saying to a companion, 'Frankly, we've never had it so good.' It was hardly a classic as newspaper cartoons go, but it was fair social comment almost a quarter of a century ago which would be just as relevant today.

A month or two later I started drawing for the *Sunday Dispatch*. I had only been working about six months when I did a drawing of removal men carrying a news editor (still at his desk) out of the office door. The news editor was looking puzzled and one of the removal men was saying to him, 'Didn't you know mate? The paper's closed down.' A few weeks later it did. I felt like the kiss of death.

In 1961 I was invited to write a humorous book on children and ponies with plenty of drawings, but I did not think that I could do it successfully. For one reason, producing captions for humorous sketches is one thing but writing a humorous book is quite another. A further problem was that even if I were capable of a piece of fairly long humorous writing which worked well in a literary sense then there seemed no point in drawing the same comic ideas as well. It seemed to me a bit like frying an egg twice. A successful cartoon may be expressed in a drawing without any caption, or it may be a drawing and a caption which are interdependent, but if the caption is a complete piece of humour there is no point in adding a drawing; in the same way, if a drawing contains a complete idea it is fatal to add words. For this reason I decided to write a simple book of instructions for pony-mad kids. No funny business – give it to them straight as if I was an expert – and then illustrate it as if I wasn't, which was true.

I called it *A Leg at Each Corner* and its significance for me was that, apart from the little book on house-hunting, it was the first book I produced from cover to cover rather than a volume composed of collected ideas which had been published before, and it became the forerunner of many more. The book was serialised in sections by the *Sunday Express* before publication and led to the character, Penelope. I had never thought of myself as a strip cartoonist and was sure that I could never cope with the repetition of a single character or group of characters. When the editor of the *Sunday Express* asked if I would like to produce one for them I had grave misgivings but decided to try it out. Strip cartoons need a title, preferably a short one which people can remember and a single name of the main character usually works best, so I called it 'Penelope', partly because it is my own daughter's name but mainly because it seemed to have the right ring for the subject-matter. I have noticed since then that the pony drawings are often referred to as the Penelope pictures, whether she appears in them or not. Her pony in the strip was called Kipper because he was half asleep when he wasn't giving her a hard time. There are a lot of children's ponies called Kipper now in the gymkhana programmes and it is very odd to read in a newspaper that a certain event was won by Fiona Jones on Thelwell. There was a racehorse, too, called Thelwell but I don't think the name did him any good: as far as I know he never made it big and I always visualised him falling asleep when he wasn't giving the jockey or the stable-lads a hard time.

He will quickly get used to having his bridle put on.

From
A Leg At Each Corner.

Don't clip him yourself unless you are an expert.

Although my drawings, particularly of the pony type, became so well known, I am not well known to the public myself; and this can lead to some odd situations. Once at a local agricultural show I heard a lady shout, 'Ha! ha! ha! Look at Thelwell – what a scream!' I froze on the spot and went goose pimples all down my back. When I had the courage to look round I saw her roaring with laughter and pointing to a minute and dishevelled child on a fat, hairy pony. The infant was giving her mount a fierce tongue-lashing whilst three red-faced ladies were trying to pull them out of the Women's Institute tent. Another time I was making some notes in a tiny sketchbook no larger than the palm of my hand when I become aware of a couple of people peeping over my shoulder. They said nothing, just watched for a short time then moved on. As they departed one said to the other, 'That chap's trying to copy Thelwell.'

Reading about one's own work in a newspaper or magazine is a strange experience. It is a combination of terror, in case they say something dreadful which would make you want to buy up all copies of the paper and burn them before anyone else reads it, and hope that they will say something complimentary so that you can get another copy to send to your aunt in New Zealand. I once read that I was the most English of cartoonists working at the time; the most English, that is, in style and subject-matter and I was very flattered. On reflection I decided that if the writer was correct there was not much hope for me overseas. Still, being English might be good for sales in England, and a few things might trickle over the border into Wales and Scotland. Oddly enough things haven't developed like that at all. My books have been translated into many different languages and I get letters from readers all over the world which I find a delightful bonus.

I was particularly surprised some years ago when someone sent me a copy of the programme for the Prague Horse Show which was illustrated throughout with my drawings. It was pleasing to see that my work was percolating through a chink in the Iron Curtain. Unfortunately, it was that very day that the Russian tanks rolled into Czechoslovakia and took over. Believe it or not the Kremlin boys never paid up. Just in case anyone should think that my grouse is politically motivated, I am bound to add that someone else sent me a very nicely laid-out pamphlet from the USA advertising the products of 'Thelwell Productions Incorporated of New York', an organisation which I had never heard of before and the President did not bother to send the Feds in to sort that lot out either.

I am pleased to say that exports to the USA are now handled in a totally satisfactory manner and that the T-shirts and other items imported from Japan, which were decorated with my drawings but without my permission, have ceased to flow in to rival the home-grown product. I must admit that I was surprised to find that the Japanese are interested in my work and pleased too, of course, particularly now that previous problems have been ironed out. What is happening behind the Iron Curtain, however, I cannot say. They've probably plugged up the leak but who knows? Perhaps one day – from somewhere beyond the Urals – 'Thelwell Productions of Tashkent' will emerge.

It's great fun having a cupboard full of one's own books which one cannot read. I'm too old now to start learning Finnish or Dutch or Danish but I think my favourite volume is the Japanese version of my book on angling which is called *The Compleat Tangler*. The Japanese title is

ザ・コンプリート・タングラー

Sort that one out!

ADDIS ABABA, 11/9/1964

DEAR MR. THELWELL,

SINCE I FIRST SAW YOUR DRAWING IN > PUNCH <
APRIL 20, 1960 ("BEARINGS DRY AS DUST! CARBURETTORS
FLOODED! IT'S RUINATION!") THE FILE WITH YOUR
AMUSING SKETCHES JEERING AT THE PARADOXICAL WAY
OF MODERN FARM LIFE HAS GATHERED A REMARKABLE
VOLUME. WATCHING THE OUTBREAKS OF PUBLIC OPINION
ABOUT AGRICULTURAL PROBLEMS VERY CAREFULLY,
I MUST CONFESS, THAT THERE IS - AS FAR AS I CAN SEE -
NO COMPARABLE CONTRIBUTION IN ANY OTHER (EUROPEAN)
SATIRICAL PERIODICAL WHICH IS AS WELL CHARACTERIZED
BY " KNOWING THE MATTER" AS BECOMES OBVIOUS IN
YOUR DRAWINGS. THE DETAILS SHOWN IN THE SKETCHES CON-
CERNING FARM EQUIPMENT LET EXPECT YOU TO HAVE WORKED
WITH BEFORE GIVING THEM A FIGURE. IN MANY OTHER SKETCHES
PUBLICATED THE UNREALISTIC AND TRADITIONAL POINT OF VIEW
OF MODERN RURAL LIFE IS UNDERLINED BY AN UNPRECISE
STYLE OF DRAWING.
PREPARING AN ANALYSIS OF THE FOUNDATED ENGLISH (PUNCH)
CRITICISM OF THE ROCKETING RURAL DEVELOPMENT, I WOULD
BE GRATEFUL TO YOU GIVING ME SOME INDICATION
HOW TO EXPLAIN THIS REFRESHING OBJECTIVITY.

YOURS SINCERELY

Dr. R. J. Böhm

An interesting spin-off from my work is receiving letters from readers, often from remote and unlikely parts of the world. I do my best to reply to all letters but sometimes it is difficult to know how to answer the questions writers ask. I once did a drawing in Punch of an experimental farm. A large pig had startled a passer-by by sticking his head over the wall and shouting 'Eureka!' A gentleman from New England wrote, 'For God's sake tell me what the joke is. It's driving me mad.' I wrote back saying, 'I don't know – it's driving me mad too!'

Another Punch drawing showed a pet shop with every kind of pet imaginable on view. A notice on the door said 'Closed for lunch' and the shopkeeper had taken one single bite from a sandwich. Every eye in the place was focused on the sandwich. There was no caption. A lady from a place called Far Forest wrote saying that she had always thought of me as an animal lover but had changed her mind since the animals in the pet shop were obviously not fed properly. Could I assure her that they had been fed since, as she could not sleep for worrying about them. A few days later I had a letter from Herbert Marshall, one of the famous enclave of British actors in Hollywood. He enclosed forty dollars and hoped it would be enough to buy the original of the pet-shop drawing. 'The funniest thing I've seen for years,' he wrote.

On another occasion a gentleman wrote saying that he and his colleagues enjoyed my work and added, 'If you are ever near here please drop in and see us. You will be most welcome.' The address was the Department of Oceanography, Honolulu University.

A lady once wrote from South Africa. Her parents were English, she said, and although she had been born in Africa she had always thought of England as home. Recently she had spent a holiday in England and had bought my book Thelwell Country as a souvenir. 'When I look at it here in Bloemfontein,' she said, 'it brings tears to my eyes.' I foolishly showed the letter to an artist friend of mine. 'No bloody wonder,' he said, 'the way you draw!'

I have been asked on many occasions whether it annoys or distresses me that my name is associated in the public mind with children on ponies when, in fact, they have been a relatively small part of my work. Sometimes I have the feeling that the inquisitors are a little deflated when I say no. This may be because things which go smoothly are usually much less interesting than things which go wildly wrong. As a cartoonist I understand this phenomenon. It is a similar question to 'Did winning the pools bring you happiness or did it ruin your life?' It is far more interesting to those who have never won anything in their lives to hear that the filthy lucre brought the recipient to wild dissipation and ultimate misery. After all, it is strangely comforting to be assured that luck does not bring happiness, at least until one fills in the next pools coupon. I have read that some artists have resented the fact that the public link their names forever with some highly popular and successful work they produced earlier in their careers. I know what they mean. They mean that, whilst they were pleased at the time to produce work which made their names well known to the public and their financial situation rather more comfortable, they now wish to gain equal recognition for work which they feel to be on a higher plane. It seems to me to be a very worthy ambition and essential to any artist's progress. But success will surely depend on the quality of the work they continue to produce and not on their loudly condemning their own earlier work.

I'm quite sure that there are many excellent artists who would not be averse to stumbling upon something which caught the popular imagination – and I use the word stumbling advisedly, for my life as an artist has been one long stumble. The fact is that any artist worth his or her salt is never satisfied with their own work once it is finished. I am aware that there is something deep in the human psyche that makes all of us want to do something or leave something behind that will establish the fact that we once lived on this earth. This is why first-year students in art schools love to talk about 'painting for posterity'. It is why

lovers carve their initials on trees and graffiti merchants scribble on walls. It is the one and only reason why 'Kilroy was here'. One is hardly likely ever to know what posterity will think, but I have greatly enjoyed receiving hundreds of letters, some from the remotest parts of the earth, from people who have enjoyed something that I have done in the essential loneliness of my own workroom.

Throughout the sixties I devoted two or three days each week to drawings for *Punch*. Producing ideas was always much more difficult than doing the final drawings. The system was to spend one or two days on ideas and hope to get five or six likely notions drawn up as 'roughs'. These were usually drawn on fairly flimsy paper in pencil only and sent to the art editor. If things went well the roughs would be returned a day or two later with one or perhaps even two of the sketches marked 'OK – half-page' or 'OK – small'. Sometimes, although to be truthful not very often, they would be returned with a rejection slip. This could be a bit depressing if one had had a hard time finding the ideas. On the other hand the rejection slips from *Punch* were usually softened by a pencilled remark such as 'Sorry, not quite' initialled by the art editor. Rejected roughs could, of course, be submitted to other magazines and it was quite possible that an idea would be bought by the second, third or even fourth publication it was sent to. Rejected ideas can sometimes be sold later to the magazine which rejected them. Editors are only human, after all, and an idea which does not appeal to them one day may well strike a chord at a later date. I have known a small black-and-white drawing of mine to be rejected and then to be accepted by the same magazine later as a front cover in colour at more than ten times the price.

WHAT DATE DO WE OPEN TO THE PUBLIC ? "

'What date do we open to the public?'

"IT'S NOTHING SERIOUS, DOCTOR. I'M JUST NOT FEELING SUPERIOR, THATS ALL."

'It's nothing serious, doctor. I'm just not feeling superior, that's all.'

Rough pencil sketches submitted to Punch *and the finished drawings as they appeared in the magazine.*

THE
EFFLUENT
SOCIETY

METHUEN & CO LTD

Although my object as a cartoonist was mainly to earn my living by amusing readers, it was also quite possible to express my own feelings on subjects, situations and events about which I felt strongly. Politics I have always found very boring and there was no way in which I could have become a political cartoonist. My interest lies in the minutiae of the human dilemma, the day-to-day problems of life and the way we are all swept along by events or developments which we feel helpless to influence. I seem to have touched at one time or another on almost every subject under the sun from combine harvesters to computers, rockets to ramblers, paraffin to pigs. But the predominant thread which has always run through my work is my love of and fascination with the countryside: the flesh and bones of these islands.

(below and left) From *Punch* and *The Effluent Society*.

'Run for it. The water main's burst.'

'So far I've spotted 13 hedgehogs, 4 rabbits, a squirrel, 3 rooks, a chaffinch and a pied wagtail.'

(above and opposite) From *Punch* and *The Effluent Society*.

'Run along and help Grandad freeze the chickens!'

'He loves feeding the chickens.'

After the war there were bound to be great
changes in Britain. Heaven knows they were
needed, and I wanted them as much as anyone. It
was all very simple to me then; black was black
and white was white and shades of grey were
merely prevarication. But of course I soon
discovered that few things in life are simple. The
problem is that whilst one certainly cannot make
an omelette without breaking eggs, if the omelette
is uneatable the eggs are no longer there. What
seems at first sight like prevarication may possibly
be the time required for careful thought and
preparation, and all of life is in various shades and
colours. Black and white are almost non-existent.

Suddenly Britain seemed to be full of men on
bulldozers revving powerful engines in a haze of
blue smoke and looking about them in a frenzy for
something to knock down. There was undoubtedly
a great deal which needed knocking down,
provided that it was going to be replaced by
something better, but I was horrified by the
indiscriminate way that many of our buildings and
much of our landscape was destroyed. The little
ponds where cattle drank and we children
discovered the wonder and delight of the natural
world were filled in to produce a few more square
feet of crops. Hundreds of miles of hedgerows,
which had taken hundreds of years to mature, were
ripped out to make way for ever bigger farm
machines. Small spinneys and copses, the last
refuge for many wild creatures, fell in a matter of
hours to whining chain-saws and caterpillar
tractors in the name of progress and efficiency.
Before the boom in country property values
occurred in the sixties, many cottages, smithies,
shops and schools, which had come into being to
serve the now redundant farmworkers, were left to
rot or were knocked down. The soft warm farms
of England were replaced or surrounded by shiny
metal monstrosities as offensive to the eye as a tin
can on a Persian carpet.

It was much the same in our towns and cities,
which were disembowelled and their populations
transported to terrifying tower blocks or sent to
live in the soulless, often jerry-built sprawl of

*In 1976 a large tract of water meadows
bordering the River Test was sold to a
gravel company without the knowledge of
most of the local residents. There was
already considerable gravel-digging activity in the area and the news of further
despoliation was a severe shock. Not only
was another large area of the Test Valley
threatened with destruction but if it was
allowed to continue it was difficult to see
where it would all end. There was at
that time great alarm and determined
resistance to various schemes for the development of roads and fly-overs in the
Winchester area and one could not help
but feel that we were about to see the
Test Valley torn up to win gravel so that
it could be turned into concrete and
poured all over the equally beautiful
Itchen Valley.*

*I was so alarmed that I stayed up all
night, completed this poster before breakfast and had 500 copies printed within a
few days. Many people were involved in
the organised protests which quickly followed and the posters were widely distributed and displayed in house and shop
windows, on gates, fences and in local
newspapers and (I was pleased to see)
even in the local government offices at
Romsey. Happily, permission to dig up
the water meadows for gravel was finally
refused and the land was returned to
farming. I like to think that the poster
played some small part in bringing about
such a satisfactory conclusion.*

*It was subsequently published in a
number of magazines and the drawing
has since been used as far away as Brazil
in similar campaigns to protect some of
the natural beauty of our planet.*

SAVE THE TEST VALLEY

STOP THE GRAVEL VANDALS

Church at Tremezzo on Lake Como.
Sketchbook page 11″ × 8″.

Esino Iario. Sketchbook page 11″ × 8″.

Winchester Cathedral from Badgers Farm.
Water-colour 15″ × 21″.

Salisbury Cathedral from Harnham Mill.
Water-colour 15″ × 21″.

hen-houses and rabbit hutches which were being thrown up round some of our delightful country towns, thus destroying their charm and character forever.

But all of this could be defended by logical argument. Who needed ponds when water could be carried to drinking troughs by polythene tubes? Was it not true that the whole world needed as much cheap food as possible and were blackberries and butterflies to stand in the way of combines and silage towers? Of course not. Was not hygienically wrapped and ready-sliced bread for all, even if it did look and taste like plastic, more important than sweet bryony and wild roses? It takes time and money and care to cure the damp and mend the roofs of obsolete cottages and how were the owners to know that in a few years' time they would become 'desirable residences' worth a fortune? What does it matter if we have tin farms if they are more efficient, cheaper to build and maintain and easier to run than stone and timber ones? Cows and pigs and hens can live indoors out of the wind and rain and have their food brought to them on conveyor belts and . . . what is wrong with rehousing underprivileged people in nice clean concrete towers with their own indoor lavatory and wall-to-wall happiness?

Like many other people, I had the feeling that the planners and developers could not see, or chose to ignore, the maggots in the apple and I took the opportunity to say so graphically whenever the opportunity presented itself. One or two people suggested that my attacks were too gentle and that I should put more acid in my ink, but that was not the way I wanted to do it. I have known many farmers in my time and several are among my best and closest friends. They are not monsters, as they were sometimes depicted to be when the anti-factory farming bandwagon began to roll. It seems to me that to represent them as such is not only unfair but seriously weakens the point that one is trying to make. To some extent, at least, this was true for most of the people who were changing the face of Britain and I have always taken the view that it is better to deal with a problem from a more oblique angle than bashing it straight in the face. The trouble with going into the attack with all guns blazing is that it leaves very little in one's armoury after the first salvos, and rabid aggression tends to lose sympathy for any cause.

My angle has always been to try to point out the sad results of what I feel to be mistaken attitudes. Ridicule, I am convinced, is often a far more powerful weapon than a gun. At the end of the sixties I decided to do a book on the subject of what we were doing to the world we live in. I wanted to deal with pollution of the earth, the air, our rivers and the sea. I wanted to bring in the prevalent habit of dumping waste material, from wrecked cars to atomic waste; the escalating horrors of factory farming; wholesale destruction of wild-life; computerisation; over-population; tower-block housing; protest marchers and the rest. I knew I had done quite a lot, mostly in the pages of *Punch*, on most of these subjects but I did not realise that when I went through the work I had already done I would have more than enough material to fill all ninety-six pages of the book I had planned. I've done books on a whole range of subjects but none has given me more personal satisfaction than *The Effluent Society*.

From *Punch* and *The Effluent Society*.

9: PHANTOMS, FLINTS AND MILLSTONE GRIT

Derelict Cottages, Hampshire. Water-colour 10″ × 15″.

We had been living at Cherry Hill for about five years when I found myself suddenly faced with the challenge of turning my theories about conservation into action. When we bought the house, the package included a pair of semi-detached cottages within the grounds which, although they were occupied by a man and his wife on the one side and a mother and her two teenage children on the other, were not in truth in a fit state to house animals. Like so many of the rural slums which existed all over the countryside until after the Second World War, however, they were picturesque and added a good deal of visual charm

to that part of the village. But the facts were grim. The roof was rotten and leaking, the walls were damp and every bit of woodwork was suffering from wet or dry rot or woodworm. Sanitation was catered for by two tiny tumble-down earth closets outside.

Both dwellings consisted of one room upstairs and one down, connected by a small almost spiral staircase tucked into the corners of the building, and the upper room of one cottage, occupied by the mother and teenage children (of different sexes), was divided in two only by a flimsy studwork screen. Each cottage had a cramped

(above) Sketchbook page.

(right) Pencil sketches: *(above) Lynhay Meads, Hampshire*; *(below) South Wales Valley.*

lean-to wooden shed with a tap but only one had a sink. With electric light these were the only signs of convenience. There was no question of us profiting in any way by owning these cottages but technically we were landlords and it caused us considerable anguish. Both families had lived in the building for many years and it was difficult to know how to act without seeming either to be interfering with their privacy or to be indifferent to their plight.

I contacted several builders but they flatly refused to touch the cottages. They were close to collapse, they said, and were not prepared to take the risk of climbing onto the roof. Nothing could be done whilst the place was occupied and in their opinion once they were vacated the only sensible course was to knock them down. I thought of making strong protests to the local authority and pointing out that the two families were in dire need of rehousing but I was worried that any great pressure on my part might be misinterpreted as an attempt to get the tenants out for my own convenience or profit. I did in fact contact them after some hesitation because the health of one lady was causing much concern and I was relieved· to find that the authorities agreed with me and promised to do their best.

Our peace of mind was not improved either by the man whose wife was so ill. He was an inoffensive and friendly enough fellow with whom I often chatted in the evening over the garden gate. He never made any comment about me being the technical owner of the property in which he lived but he would sometimes nod towards another cottage on the other side of the lane which was in a similar state of delapidation to his own. That heap of ruin and decay had also been bought by a stranger to the village, who eventually restored it to a delightful sound and well-appointed home which was an asset in both a visual and practical sense to the village. 'That's the trouble you see,' he would say. 'These people come along and buy up our homes and there's nothing left for the likes of us.' There was no rancour in the man, however, and we always remained on excellent terms, although I

knew he was obliquely referring to me as well as a number of other newcomers.

Rhona and I were very concerned, as the health of his wife was clearly deteriorating, but we were powerless to solve the problem in a satisfactory way. At that time we were renewing the roof on our own house and modernising the antiquated facilities within. There was in consequence a yard full of building materials – bricks, tiles, slates and many household objects such as pipes, taps, a bath, two deep ceramic sinks, lavatory basins, etc., which, if old-fashioned, were none the less in excellent condition. They lay near the end of my neighbour's garden not more than fifty paces at most from his cottage door. Unlike his wife he was in good health and only in his middle years.

'Why don't you take one of these sinks?' I said to him. 'There are bricks here, too, which you are welcome to and the builders mix fresh mortar and cement almost every day. If you set aside a Saturday morning you could build two brick supports and have a sink in place by midday. All the fittings are there too, and if you give me a shout I'll help you carry the stuff.'

He shuffled his feet and said, 'We've only got a bucket under the tap, you know. It's hard for my wife. What can you do when you only have a bucket under the tap?'

'Put a sink under it,' I said.

But he appeared not to hear and told me a sad little story of how a man had died in some mysterious way after jumping off the crumbling flint wall near which we were standing. His shiftless attitude was a puzzle to me but when I reflected on the appalling conditions in which he had lived for many years I began to wonder whether if I had lived in similar circumstances I might not also have been reduced to such apathy.

We were much relieved when the two families were rehoused and the authorities issued a demolition order on the cottages. But if I sat by and watched them fall to the bulldozers the character of that part of the village would change overnight and I could not visualise another house which would fit into its surroundings so well. I

The Tide-mill at Beaulieu. Pencil.

Bayards Cove, Dartmouth. Pen-and-ink sketch.

needed time to think so I asked for stay of execution and was given a year's grace to come up with a solution. Rhona and I worked almost every evening during that year making plans and drawings of what might possibly be done to avoid demolition.

It was obvious that no more than the outer walls could be saved and the building was too small to be practical for present day living so that it would have to be enlarged. The problem was how to do it without destroying its character. I had seen a number of attempts to enlarge cottages by sticking on new pieces but the results were always a disaster. There was already one in the village which looked as if a modern electric train had run into the side of an old steam locomotive. Our cottages were built of flint with soft red-brick corners and window surrounds, and I was determined to carry out all new work in the same style and with the same kind of materials. It was then that I hit the first snag. All new work would, quite rightly, have to conform to modern standards and I could not find a builder who had built or heard of anyone else building cavity walls in flint. They said it was not possible but when I asked why they didn't seem to have an answer. 'It just can't be done,' they said. I'm sure they thought I was either a pest or a loony. I finally talked to a man who had never heard of it being done before but who was quite happy to try anything once. He grinned, shrugged his shoulders and said, 'It's your money you're risking.' The planning authority probably grinned and shrugged too but they passed my plans and work was started.

The interior layer of the walling was built in the normal manner with conventional materials. I was able to get matching brick from the local brickworks for the corners and window and door surrounds, and a good supply of the soft red hand-made tiles which at that time were being thrown from the roofs of cottages all over the south of England and exploding in red dust to be swept away with the stone and oak beams by advancing bulldozers. The outer walls of the cottage extensions were built of flints which were laid with mortar inside wooden shuttering. Wall ties were inserted in the usual way and, provided that the flints were laid to no more than a two-feet depth at a time and the shuttering was left in place for a day or two before being raised to take the next section, the work was straightforward. We did not meet any special difficulties whatsoever.

When the shuttering was removed the strip of wall which was exposed looked very messy because the mortar had spread over most of the flint facing. The mortar had, however, reached a 'green' stage by then which meant that although it was firm and strong, it had not become really hard and it was quite possible to cut, carve or scrape it so that each individual flint was exposed. I prefer the pleasant buff, white and yellow-ochre colours of flint surfaces to the rather grey effect which knapped flint produces, so that as the walls moved upwards the textures and colours were very pleasant. Both Rhona and I, and David and Penny, tried carving the mortar between the stones and we found it to be an absorbing and relaxing occupation. So much so, in fact, that there was keen competition to get at the next section of wall. Penny had collected one or two stones which pleased her eye at each place she had visited since infancy and she kept them in her bedroom, neatly displayed like jewellery. The lure of the walls however was too much for her and one by one she produced her treasures to be incorporated in the pattern. When the work was complete she was able to point out her own stones and recount their history. (When we were leaving Braishfield later, however, she asked for her stones to be returned. We dried her tears and explained that however loudly she howled the stones could not be recovered. It did not prevent her having a go at those she could reach.)

The finished design of the cottage was pleasantly irregular in shape and the roofing was almost as much of a challenge as the walls. I had managed to buy, and thus rescue, 22,000 hand-made tiles, many of them with their wooden pegs still in place, which would otherwise have been destroyed. When the whole job was

Cottages at Merthyr Mawr, South Wales.
Fountain pen and wet-thumb sketch.

Lacock Abbey, Wiltshire. Pen-and-ink and wash.

completed there were only a few thousand left over and every one which remained undamaged has been used since then. Those tiles were made in 1788. I found one of them on which that date had been cut several times when the clay was wet. Two men had also signed their names and thus ensured their immortality for at least two hundred years. I still have that tile in my workroom and another one which is inscribed with a simple sum, with a grand total of £3. 2s. 0d. Perhaps it was the wages list for the week. One thing at least I know about James Brown and William Fance: they could produce a quite elegant copper-plate hand even with the point of a trowel. It is rather more information than one can gather from 'Kilroy was here'.

It is strange, the apparent tendency of human beings to destroy things first and think after. Hundreds of thousands of those lovely roof tiles must have been destroyed during the fifties and sixties, and heaven knows what else, in the mad rush to build a better world; and now those that remain are so scarce that they are at a premium if they are obtainable at all. It is by no means a new phenomenon, nor is it confined to any particular group or class. I recall that when I was a child in Birkenhead I had a great-aunt and uncle who were coal merchants. I say 'they' were coal merchants because Aunt Amelia (a generously built woman) worked just as hard in their small coalyard as Uncle Tom did. I can see her now swilling the cement floor with a hosepipe and scrubbing it vigorously with a yard brush right up to the heaps of coal until it was all clean and tidy. It mattered not one jot to her that the next load of coal to come in or go out would cover the place with coaldust again; she would simply go out there and scrub it down again. I wanted to ask her why she did it but she was a woman not to be trifled with and I never found the courage. At least I suppose she had slightly more success than King Canute. Their business was little more than a subsistence living and when they became old they seemed to have almost nothing. Nothing, that is, except a collection of china which seemed to me then to fill their otherwise dismal little house. I know now that

it consisted mainly of old Staffordshire ware but I simply remember it as a treasure-house of timeless dogs staring into space with gold chains about their necks, kings and heroes on horseback, colourful soldiers and animals and groups of figures of all kinds. I went with my mother one day to visit them. They were sitting there as always, one each side of the fire-grate, but the pottery and china were gone. It seemed to me that what little light they had in their house had been turned out.

'Where is all your lovely china, Auntie?' asked my mother.

'I tipped the lot into the dustbin, Emmy,' she said. 'I can't be bothered cleaning all that stuff any more.'

I remember wondering why she had not saved just a little of the energy she had expended on the floor of the coalyard to lavish on her treasures; but in those days children, we were reliably informed, should be seen and not heard.

Prodigality is not confined to the downtrodden, however. A man who was doing a job for me in the garden a few years ago told me that he was once employed with two other men for a whole year to burn a million railway sleepers. I was recently looking for railway sleepers to build a small footbridge over a stream and they now cost anything from eight to ten pounds each if one can get them. It is a fair guess that they will cost more as they get scarcer. One way or another eight to ten million pounds' worth of railway sleepers would be enough to keep Fleet Street in bingo prizes for some time.

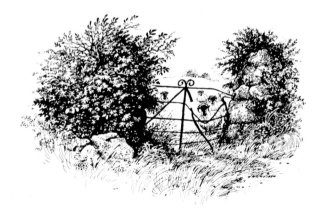

Deserted Cottage on Bodmin Moor.
Water-colour 10″ × 12″.

(left) From *A Millstone Round My Neck.* Pen and ink.

From *A Millstone Round My Neck.*

When the cottage was finished it was so beautiful that we decided to move into it and lease Cherry Hill. It was a much simpler affair than moving into the bungalow at Codsall. For one thing it was in our own garden, no more than fifty yards away. We could move our furniture in without going out of our own front gate. The only snag was that a pantechnicon would clearly be a waste of time and money when each piece could be carried across the lawn by hand. I learned something else about human preferences that day. Removal men, on the whole, prefer to stagger out of a house with pieces of furniture and put them straight into their vehicle, then have a few quiet cups of tea and a nice long drive before taking them out again. They do not seem to enjoy staggering out and then staggering fifty yards before they stagger straight into the new house without a tea-break. For one thing, they have to carry the heavy bits much further that way and, as it is clearly a waste of time to pack all the lighter stuff, they have to drape it all under their arms and over their shoulders and on their heads and walk about in public view looking like real Charlies. When they were down to the really light stuff I gave them a hand and on the way up the slope I met one of them on the way down. He was carrying so many house plants that he looked like an animated bush. I wouldn't have put him down as a great reader of the classics to be honest but he startled me as we drew level by pushing his head out of the foliage and saying, 'Hey, guv! Which way to Dunsinane?'

There was a minor crisis when his mate came running into the cottage looking as if he was in shock.

'Did you know one of the bedrooms is full of dead birds?' he asked, rubbing his hands down his coat as if he'd just put them into something nasty.

'Oh, they're David's specimens,' we said. 'Put them into the end bedroom and let him sort them out.' He hesitated, looking as if he couldn't believe his ears. 'A pile of them fell out of the piano stool as well,' he said.

'Oh dear, I keep asking him not to keep them

there,' said Rhona. 'Never mind. If they get mixed up it's his own fault. Just put them with the others.'

By the time they were having a cup of tea we thought we had better explain the dead birds so we told them that David had been a mad-keen ornithologist since he was about five years old and had noticed that all the sparrows in the garden did not look exactly the same. As soon as we explained that they were not all sparrows he had been launched into a life-long interest and had been making drawings of them whenever he could get one to keep still. The only wild birds that will keep still long enough to be drawn in any detail are usually dead so whenever a neighbour found a dead bird in their garden they would bring it round for him to draw. We went on to explain that the birds in his bookshelves and (as far as we knew) those in the piano stool were stuffed by some reasonably competent taxidermist and that David had arrived home from school with a cargo of them when the natural history section of the school museum was having a clear out. We were relieved to find that all we had to do to keep those removal men happy was to explain away our children's collection of interesting bits of tree branch, stones, shells and dead birds. It was little enough trouble compared with my problems at Codsall, trying to sort out a feud between removal men and lethargic builders when suffering from all-over housemaid's knee.

The Bridge at Rhayader, Mid-Wales.

The Eel-trap Bridge on the Test.

My interest in old and beautiful buildings was by now getting a bit complicated and I must back-track to get things straight (in my own mind that is). Cherry Hill had been more or less sorted out, the soggy slopes had been terraced with about thirty tons of dry walling (by me I hasten to add). There were about another thirty tons covered with nettles waiting to be used round the cottages which at that time were only about two thirds of the way to completion when Rhona asked me if I was interested in an old mill by a stream. Her question was put to me one Sunday evening at a period when I was trying to cope with more freelance work than I could comfortably handle, get on with

dry walling, supervise the building of the cottage and fit in as much trout fishing as possible. I was also worrying about my dandruff and the fact that I was failing to flip through the colour supplements before they were used to light the fire.

'Where is it?' I asked.

'In Cornwall,' she said and read the whole item to me from the 'Property for Sale' column. 'Picturesque water-mill . . . three-bedroomed cottage attached . . . stretch of salmon and trout river . . . mill leat . . . cider press . . . range of outbuildings . . . delightful wooded valley . . . needs some attention.'

Buildings in the Mill Yard. From *A Millstone Round My Neck.*

Well, there was no harm in looking, was there? So we drove to Cornwall very early the next morning and after some searching we eventually located the mill. It was in a very neglected condition and only the great strength of its granite construction saved it from being derelict. The mill itself had a *Marie Celeste* air about it. The machinery was more or less intact and personal objects and hand tools lay about in the dust as if laid down for a moment and never taken up again due to some sudden, nameless catastrophe. The mill was in three storeys, but the cottage which was linked to it was only in two and both were in worse condition than the mill. There was a shippen with standing for two cows built onto the end of the cottage in the same heavy granite blocks but the range of outbuildings had reached a point of disintegration, so textured and colourful with rust, lichen and mould that to a painter's eye they were quite beautiful.

At the time I could never have explained to anyone why I bought it. I couldn't explain it to myself either when I thought of all the things I already had on my plate. But I think it had something to do with the fact that mills represent man's very earliest effort to organise himself into an ordered and progressive way of life. They are elemental and timeless, although their time, it seemed, had run out. But partly it was the river that tumbled past with wild trout in its fast runnels, the hundreds of pale yellow primroses that trembled in the grass among the rocks and the wild daffodils blowing beneath the orchard trees. It was also the cider press beneath a roof held up by megolithic slabs of granite, the sound of the mill leat pouring through the long-still water-wheel and the buzzards circling in the high blue dome of the sky.

During the following three or four years the mill was the source of much discomfort and many quiet pleasures. We spent days of grinding hard work and days of languid fishing along the river. We drove down there through sheeting rain and darkness, through morning mist and sunshine. We wondered often why we had taken on the task of saving the place from ruin when we were driven out into the rainy night by chimneys that sucked smoke downwards, springs that ceased to flow, pumps that kept us wakeful through the early hours and sheep that rolled onto their backs and had to be turned over with the yardbrush before breakfast. But we got our answer when the wheel turned once more on the mill wall, when the glow-worms were like scattered sparks among the wayside fuchsias on summer evenings and when the smell of breakfast bacon frying drifted out from the kitchen door and the clean, fresh scents of the valley drifted in.

We had many hours of pleasure there, not only around the mill itself but on fishing trips along the river with angling friends and painting weekends along the valley and up on the wild and lonely moor among the cairns and engine houses. Simple experiences they were, which we had enjoyed in other parts of England too, but Cornwall is different. Inland there is an atmosphere of potent, brooding mystery which cannot be ignored or forgotten. It is a land of legend where myth is more powerful than fact and one can feel it in the rocks, in the coarse moorland grasses bending in the wind, in farms and buildings, in the ancient stone circles and in the very air itself.

This atmosphere hung about the old mill like a magnetic field round an iron core. The mill drew me to itself and yet it held aloof. The granite pile could be warm and friendly sometimes on balmy summer days, in spite of the feeling I always had that its past inhabitants had never quite left it; but when the weather changed and charcoal grey clouds dragged their ragged edges across the sky it could be sulky and withdrawn or charged with vague menace.

I can remember every detail of the mill at Penruin as if I had been there only yesterday but without question it was its atmosphere which impressed itself most strongly upon my mind. I never discussed this with Rhona or the children in case it put them off the place, for I was aware that they were less strongly drawn to it than I was, but, partly due to this and partly to the fact that it was too remote to be convenient for the work I was doing at that time, it was impossible to live there permanently. We didn't own it long enough to complete the work we started but we have never regretted the work we did. When we first saw it it was a beautiful ruin but when we left it was just as picturesque but was a ruin no longer. We did not restore it as fully as we would have wished but we stopped the rot in more ways than one.

When I felt it safe to do so I asked Rhona, the children and all the friends who spent fishing or painting weekends there with me whether they noticed any atmosphere. They had all been aware of it, it seemed, but had decided to be diplomatic and keep quiet. I am in no way psychic, nor have I ever had a mystical experience of any kind; and on the whole, although I like to think that I keep an open mind on all subjects, I must admit to being sceptical about such matters. But when we visited the mill again some years later we were told of an accident years before when a man became entangled in those great gears which turned the millstones. We didn't get the whole story, unfortunately, but it made us wonder again about the dusty hand-tools that lay about the place when we first saw it, the old coat on the rail by the door and the boots, nibbled by mice, that were in the corner of the upper floor.

My liking for watermills is shared by many other people, it seems: in May 1966 I wrote a short article about Penruin in the *Sunday Express* and I was amazed by the number of letters which I got from readers. They were by no means restricted to enthusiasts with a passion for industrial archaeology either; my impression was that most people who wrote were dreamers – and why not? I am surprised by the way that the word 'escapism' is so often used in a derogatory way nowadays, as if the user imagines himself to be superior to those who love literature, painting, music, religion, poetry and entertainment of every kind; for can they not all be lumped together as escapism by those whose minds are so arid that they can appreciate only the ugliness of existence?

That small article about our mill revealed also a most unexpected coincidence. A lady wrote to me to say that people had been calling at her house after reading it and asking whether they could look around. It happened that she and her husband owned a watermill – in Cornwall – and their name was also Thelwell. There are not all that many of us about and we visited each other's mills shortly after. As far as we could tell there were no other people of that name in Cornwall when we met but another family arrived shortly after; and although we never worked out how we were related, we had a 'family' gathering – and great fun it was.

Many people thought that I was crazy to get involved with a watermill while we were only about three-quarters of the way to completing the rebuilding of the cottages at Braishfield in Hampshire. The truth is that the same thought passed through my own mind more often than I would have liked to admit. But the world was young in the sixties and vibrant with a spirit of experiment and adventure. I was younger, too, of course, and perhaps that is why I could cope with the complications and discomforts, as well as taking such delight in the excitement of new ventures. Besides which, I had never neglected the more serious side of my drawing and painting and the mill at Penruin was grist to my pen and brush, as indeed was almost every part of Cornwall.

Cornish Watermill. Water-colour 15″ × 21″.

Early Morning, Brixham. Water-colour 15″ × 21″.

Ducks on the Pond at Herons Mead. Pastel sketch.

Fishing-boats off the Dart. Water-colour 10″ × 14″.

Sheep Farm in Mid-Wales.

We returned to Hampshire quite sure that not a moment of our time at the mill had been wasted.

Our cottage in Hampshire was very different from the mill not only in a visual and practical sense but it had a quite different atmosphere. It was totally devoid of menace or mystery. There was, however, one small corner of the village which had a rather brooding air, due to tall dark trees which lined the lane on either side and mingled their great branches overhead to form a sombre green tunnel. I had heard a few stories from time to time about people who claimed to have seen a lady in a green dress there, with a very full-spreading skirt, standing in the lane in the half-light of evening. One such tale was claimed by a farm worker cycling home from the pub on a dark winter's night who said that he had come so near to running into her that he had fallen off his bicycle. These sightings, if they occurred at all, suggested that they were the product of alcoholic excess rather than any ghostly manifestations and they tended to have a decidedly comic air about them. They were all claimed to have occurred close to a large house near to the tunnel of trees and the description of the lady in green was similar in each case. I dismissed the whole thing as a village prank. For one thing, I could not imagine an inebriated farm worker who had tumbled off his bicycle after meeting a ghostly apparition describing the lady's dress as dark green taffeta, even if it had not been a pitch black night. Most men, whatever their occupation, would find it difficult to describe what their own wives were wearing the last time they saw them even when they are stone-cold sober. Furthermore, although it is many years since I saw anyone leaving a pub on a bicycle, I remember that the cycle lamps of those days did little more than cast a faint glow over the front wheel.

When we were first engaged upon clearing the rampant jungle from the house on the hill I had a good deal of help from a local countryman who was a prodigious worker and knowledgeable about all aspects of country life. He knew how to dispose of wasps' nests, how to pull down a dangerous barn, how to lay a new lawn and deal with moles that dug it up again. He was astonishingly knowledgeable about birds, flowers (both wild and cultivated), how to grow vegetables or organise the greenhouse, and a host of other useful and interesting things. He was a man who commanded respect and got it, I believe, from everyone. He was not, however, a man for tittle-tattle, tall stories or practical jokes. Although he had recently retired he had spent all his working life as gardener at the house where the green lady was said to appear from time to time. There was something about his character which made me hesitate to ask him whether he had ever seen the apparition. One afternoon when we were working together in the garden I put the question to him.

He stopped what he was doing instantly and straightened up. 'I don't like answering questions like that,' he said. 'There are too many people who ask a serious question and then when you answer them they snigger. It makes me angry,' he said.

'I'm sorry, Tom,' I said. 'I know you lived there for many years and I just thought . . . '

'I'll tell you once,' he said, cutting across my embarrassment, and he told me the following story.

He had come to the village as gardener to the house in question very soon after he had been married, but as the cottage which he and his wife were to occupy was not quite ready they had been given a bedroom at the end of a passage at the top of the house. On the first evening they were preparing to go to bed when he decided that he would visit the lavatory while his wife was doing her hair. He had stepped out into the passage and gone only a few paces when a lady in old-fashioned clothes, 'like a green crinoline' he said, had appeared in the passage coming quickly towards him. He had been surprised and embarrassed at being dressed only in his pyjamas and had pressed himself against the wall to let her pass. She went straight into the bedroom which he had just left and he expected his wife to cry out in alarm because she was a very nervous young woman. He hurried back into the room wondering what was happening and was surprised to find his

Bonfire at Mottisfont.
Water-colour 10″ × 14″.

Sketch of Hampshire cottage.

Sketchbook pages: *(above) Pentre-ty-Gwyn, pen drawing; (below) Fallen Beech In New Forest,* pencil.

wife sitting up in bed quietly doing her hair. There was no one else there, he said, and he managed to say nothing about what he had seen in case he frightened his wife.

He had not seen anything strange in the house in the next twenty years or more until one night when he was locking up. It was part of his duty before returning to his own cottage to lock and bolt the front door of the house and to close the glass doors (which had green baize on them, he said) that led to the rooms on each side of the hall. As he was pushing home the bolt on the door the dog rushed down the hall and crashed into the door beside him giving him quite a shock. He turned round to see what had startled the dog and saw the green lady coming down the staircase. She had stepped into the hall only a few paces from him and turned into one of the rooms with the glass and green baize doors. He had followed her in and found nothing.

'And that's it,' said Tom. 'I neither saw, heard nor felt anything else strange or unusual in the place all the years I worked there. Although the batman did, I'm sure of that,' he added.

'The batman?' I queried, and Tom told me the batman's story.

During the last war there was a gunsite in a field opposite the house. The lane outside the house led for some distance to the left and then turned in a half-circle to the right and continued on into the village, thus containing another small field between the house and the field where the guns were sited. There was an arrangement between the CO of the anti-aircraft unit and the owner of the house to do a friendly swap. A pheasant or two from the house to the Army and a bit of butter the other way round.

One night Tom and his wife were expecting the CO's batman to call and deliver something or pick something up when they were startled suddenly by a violent crash against the door and an urgent knocking, and when they opened up the batman almost fell into the cottage, white-faced and trembling. At first they thought he was ill but as soon as he recovered himself he told them that he had taken a short cut across the little field opposite where he had almost bumped into a woman standing quite still in the darkness. She seemed to be dressed in old-fashioned clothes, he told them. 'I don't know why I ran but she scared the hell out of me!'

Sceptical as I was about such matters, I could not imagine Tom making up the stories. He was simply not that kind of man and I really did not know what to think. The house which was said to be the centre of these supernatural events became empty and was divided by the new owner into three separate residences which he renovated and modernised before selling them again. That was the situation when we moved into our cottage and the fact that we planned to lease Cherry Hill must have become common knowledge in the village, because before we had advertised the fact a lady called upon us and asked if she and her husband could take over our house straight away. Although we had not met her before, we were aware that she and her husband had recently bought the centre section of what we had come to think of as Green Lady House, and having explained to her that our own plans were not yet complete, we were puzzled by the urgency of her manner and almost tearful insistence that they would like to move into Cherry Hill without delay. We said that we felt fairly sure that our own plans would be completed very soon and that we would let her know when they were, but it was not enough.

'Please!' she insisted. 'I cannot bear to be in that house on my own any more. As soon as my husband goes to work in the mornings I sit in the greenhouse and wait for him to come home again.' It was a difficult situation for us because we had a number of important decisions to make and we had no wish to be hurried into making the wrong ones. On the other hand we felt very sorry for the lady who was obviously very frightened and distressed.

She did not at first explain what had frightened her and we resisted the temptation to ask, for fear that it might distress her more; but she was back within a day or so pleading for us to hurry our plans because something else had happened. This time we asked her what. I suppose we were expecting another story about the green lady but she was never mentioned. It was, however, one of the most extraordinary stories I ever heard.

She had recently bought a new electric cooker and it was fitted into her kitchen in unblemished condition. She and her husband had locked up the house and gone into town to do some shopping and when they returned everything was exactly as they had left it. But they were horrified when they went into the kitchen to see that the top front corner of the cooker had been cut off. 'Chopped right off,' she said, 'as if by an axe.' There was no piece of metal or enamel chippings on the floor nor anywhere else in the house. Both she and her husband were quite certain that no one had entered the house since they left it.

There was nothing for it but to speed up our arrangements and give them a lease as quickly as we could.

It would be easy to be flippant about it all. As a cartoonist, I found that some delicious pictures went through my mind and fascinating questions posed themselves. Was the green lady the ghost of some long-dead axe-murderer in drag? Why had no one seen her with an axe when she was walking about the place? Where did she keep it? Under her green taffeta crinoline? And was it the brief glint of an axe blade that sent the batman clawing at Tom's cottage door in the dead of night? No one had ever suggested that the lady was anything other than a gentle soul and I found it difficult to imagine her going berserk and attacking an electric

cooker with a chopper. I was mentally toying with the strangeness of it all when I suddenly remembered something else.

Tom had a brother, Ray, who stayed with him from time to time. He was quite unlike Tom in character, much more volatile and talkative and he had told me that he was once helping Tom in the green-lady garden near an old, rather beautiful, thatched coach-house which is still there. They had both been in the empty building earlier in the morning and no one else had been near the garden since then, so Ray was very surprised to hear someone start chopping wood inside. The chopping was very loud and he could hear pieces of wood flying all over the place. He had asked his brother who could be in there but Tom only asked him why he didn't go and look for himself. Ray had hesitated to do so because he felt that the noise was somehow scary and he was relieved when Tom agreed to go with him. The sounds had ceased abruptly as they got to the door, Ray assured me, there was no one inside and the small amount of wood on the floor was quite undisturbed.

It struck me as strange that an axe should feature in two quite different stories and I was fascinated to read some years later, in a book about Hampshire villages, that apparitions recorded in Braishfield include an Edwardian lady said to be looking for her lost jewels. If the writer was referring to the green lady she certainly uses a strange tool to help her search for lost trinkets, and she searches in some unlikely places.

10: LANDSCAPES WITH WATER

Autumn Morning at Herons Mead. Water-colour, 10″ × 14″.

We enjoyed living in Braishfield both at Cherry Hill and at the cottage which we called Amberley but I still had the ambition to live close to a river one day. Although I liked the Cornish mill so much and the small-scale fairy-glen type of fishing which it provided, I was well aware that Rhona and our children did not seem particularly happy there and it was too far from London to be convenient for my work. Houses near to rivers in rural areas are comparatively rare, however, and I was therefore surprised when in 1967 I had the opportunity to buy a cottage and a piece of the River Test to go with it. It was no more than a

couple of miles away from where we were living, which meant that we would still be near the good friends we had in Braishfield; and I knew the river very well, not only because I had fallen into it a number of times during my Army training days, but because I had belonged to a small fishing club near Romsey for some years and loved its clear quiet waters, abundant wild flowers and fat sleek trout. Compared to Amberley or even to Cherry Hill the river cottage was a rather tatty, tumbledown building, but its setting in the golden Test valley was quite perfect and the possibilities for improving it were obvious.

We moved to our present home in March 1968 and set about the interesting task of converting it to the kind of place we wanted. When we took it over it had been in use as a farmhouse but it had originally been a pair of cottages on a large estate which were used as a 'bothy' or lodging for unmarried farm workers – much the same, I imagine, as the bunkhouse used by cowboys in the wild west. The chief problem we had to deal with was the leaking roof and we had the tiles taken off and the rafters felted before they were rehung. The northern end of the property was in a very poor state of repair and part of it had either been pulled down or fallen down of its own accord – it was difficult to tell which. We rebuilt it with as little change as possible because my own attitude towards restoration or development is that one should first of all take careful note of what is already attractive or satisfactory about either a building or a piece of landscape and then concentrate upon bringing out the full potential of what exists. Change for the sake of change rarely turns out to be better in every way and there is always the danger that it may destroy good features that existed before. Modern techniques and materials can sometimes overcome problems in the preservation and improvement of existing buildings which twenty or thirty years ago would have been almost insuperable.

The only thing I found disappointing was that although the cottage was so near to the river we could not see any water from the windows and I decided that, as it was not possible to move the building nearer to the water, I would have to bring the water nearer to the house. This was achieved by having a very large hole dug in the garden by a dragline machine and channelling the water from the river down a stream to the pool. It turned out to be the beginning of a fascination for water-gardening which has consumed many happy hours of my free time and given me great joy to this day.

Drawing cartoons for various publications was (and still is) a pleasant, well paid way of life, and I am far better known to the public for that kind of work than for my more serious paintings and drawings. I came to cartooning more or less by accident but I grew to love it, not only because it provided me with a comfortable living and gave me the opportunity to express a few of my own thoughts about the human dilemma, but also because I enjoyed the work itself and it brought me into contact with hundreds of people from almost all parts of the world who visited me or were kind enough to write and tell me that it gave them pleasure too. It did not, however, seriously curtail my almost reflex habit of drawing and painting almost everything about me and by the time I had been working on my water-garden for ten years I had collected several hundred drawings of the pool, the islands, the sluice gates, bridges and the many birds, animals, insects, flowers and fish which inhabited it.

I was quite fascinated by what happens to a simple hole in the ground when it has been in existence for just one decade. I had had so much intense pleasure from the little stretch of water that it seemed a good idea to record ten years in the life of a pond. This was partly for my own pleasure but also partly in the hope that if it were published in book form it might persuade a few other people to establish new ponds and lakes or rescue neglected ones and to counter, to some extent, the regrettable disappearance of field ponds from the English landscape; for, like the hundreds of miles of delightful hedgerows which are being ruthlessly destroyed every year in the name of the Holy Cow of economic farming, the destruction of ponds is robbing our country of yet another unique aspect of its rural charm and depriving generations of children of some of the finest centres for the introduction to and close study of natural history.

I had learned some time before that our family came originally from Thelwall in Cheshire which, according to the *Oxford Dictionary of English Place-names*, was spelled Thelewell in 1241 and its meaning was 'a pool by a plank bridge'. The second el is O E waēl: 'a weel, a deep pool, a deep still part of a river'. I have never been disposed to argue with any Oxford dictionary. The plank was there too in my garden where I crossed the small supply stream, so *A Plank Bridge by a Pool* became the title of the book. Although it records its fair share of comical minor mishaps and disasters, it was the first volume I had written which was not in itself a humorous book and the first one which was illustrated throughout with my own serious drawings.

Methuen published it in 1978 and put on a launch party in my garden which was so near to the water's edge that it almost became a literal launching. It was published in paperback in 1980. I was a little apprehensive that the public might be reluctant to buy a 'serious' book by one who was known only for humorous books and drawings but it was not so. Much to my surprise the pond book brought in more letters from readers than any individual publication of mine had done before and what I found even more remarkable was that about half of them came from overseas. They came from such widely separate places as the tiny island of Cava in Scapa Flow and Hawkes Bay in New Zealand, from Victoria, British Columbia and Hobart in Tasmania. It was pleasing to read that

From *A Plank Bridge by a Pool*.

people were digging ponds of their own after reading the book and that my modest little stretch of water was not only breeding a healthy population of insects, fish, water fowl and wild flowers, but was breeding new ponds and lakes in Britain and many more in distant parts of the world.

One Australian gentleman scared me by writing to say that my descriptions of the English countryside were so pleasing that he had decided to quit the outback and come to live in England. I was so alarmed that I wrote back by return telling him that it was sheeting with rain here and everyone was on strike anyway. He wrote back just as quickly saying he'd lent the book to a lot of his mates and they were all coming over. I think he must have been a joker. I hope he was. I have this recurring nightmare that some cold, wet winter's day there will be a knock at the door and a gang of big tough Aussies with rain dripping from their cork-fringed bush hats will be waiting to get their hands on me.

In the time which had elapsed since our Cornish adventure the whole episode had cocooned itself comfortably within my mind and remained pleasantly quiescent for some years. I think it was the rather unexpected success of *A Plank Bridge by a Pool* which made it stir itself again and demand to be brought out, savoured and enjoyed once more. My collection of drawings contained much material from the Cornwall days and if people enjoyed reading about the joys and disasters of messing about with pond water it seemed possible that they might also enjoy reading about a tumbledown watermill on a west country trout stream.

Once started, I began to enjoy writing about Penruin. I called the book *A Millstone Round My Neck.* As with the pond book, it was done partly for my own pleasure but I think the real motive was to tell all those who have only dreamed about having a millstone round their necks what a delightful burden it can be providing that you don't mind it chafing a bit here and there.

The great spur wheel,
from A Millstone Round My Neck.

If any doubt had ever existed in my mind about the importance of constantly drawing from life in sketchbooks (which it never has) then those two books would have convinced me that it is of vital importance, not only because it is excellent training for accurate observation and draughtsmanship but because from time to time the sketches themselves are usable as they exist and are usually much more potent because they have the freshness of immediate contact with the subject. My own sketchbook drawings are done almost automatically without any immediately conscious objective. They are not necessarily notes and details collected to be referred to for use in some later, more ambitious, scheme, although they may occasionally be used in that way when required.

Sketchbook drawings of donkeys in the New Forest.

Boats at Mudiford. Pen sketch.

River Trent, near Long Eaton. Pencil sketch.

Saddlers Mill, Romsey. Pencil sketch.

Suffolk Orchard. Pencil sketch.

Good paintings are like good books. They are the finished products of creative people, the rounded, polished and completed statements of what the artist has to say. Sketchbooks, on the other hand, are like diaries. They are intimate, almost secret documents which spring from private instinct and enthusiasm. They are collections of information produced by artists for their own use without the intention of communicating with others. It is little wonder, then, that they are so fascinating, for within their pages one may see far more of the artist than within his largest exhibited work. The artist drawing in his or her sketchbook feels no compulsion to hold up a mask to protect a public image.

Producing really good ideas, whether they are serious or humorous, is very hard work indeed but with persistence it can be done. It takes many years of drawing in sketchbooks to produce those delightfully lucid lines or swift, incisive shapes which can lift the heart like a chord of music. But the big challenge is the 'picture', and the really fine picture is the goal, the unattainable rainbow's end which most of us seek and so very few of us ever come near to finding. It is no matter, for the real joy and heartache is in the search and somewhere along the way we may stumble upon a minor gem which will give us pleasure enough until we push on in search of something better.

Boat Shed at Porlock Weir. Outdoor water-colour sketch.

Brixham Trawlers.
Water-colour 13″ × 20″.

Fishing-boats Going to Sea.
Water-colour 11″ × 17″.

(above left) St Andrew's Church, Timsbury.
Water-colour 7½″ × 9½″.

(above) Trout Stream at Herons Mead.
Water-colour 11″ × 8″.

(left) This painting was done in aid of
the Romsey Abbey Restoration Fund.
The money was raised by the sale
of a signed, limited edition of
500 colour prints.
Water-colour 13″ × 20″.

More than thirty years of working on humorous drawings and paintings may have reduced the time available for my efforts to paint a few good pictures but they have in no way diminished my desire to do so. Time does not matter anyway, for a hundred years would still be too little time to spend painting and I have after all had the pleasure also of pursuing the equally elusive and delightful subject of humour. I doubt very much whether, if I had spent my whole career as a 'serious painter', my work would have paid me so well, enabled me to live in such modestly delightful surroundings and still left me free to spend so many hours simply painting for the sheer delight of doing so and without the restriction of working to produce saleable gallery pictures. I have sold very few serious paintings. Those which escape the dustbin I keep in my own little gallery and look through from time to time to see if I am making any progress at all. At times it can be a sad business. I think that many artists would agree that the best of their pictures which have for one reason or another remained in their own possession gradually become a little like their own children. They may also become redolent of certain periods of their lives – indeed for all their faults and shortcomings they become part of one's existence, and one wants to hold onto them like a faded photograph or a comfortable old jacket.

The Beach at Beer, South Devon. Water-colour 6″ × 8″.

Eilean Donan Castle, Loch Duich, Scotland.
Water-colour and body colour 19″ × 12″.

Farm on Bodmin Moor, Cornwall.
Water-colour 10″ × 14½″.

169

I have always held the view that the professional artist who has to wait for 'inspiration' before he can get down to work is a prime candidate for one of Mrs Thatcher's retraining schemes. The basic requirements, apart from a certain ability to draw and paint, are to develop a wide interest in the world about us and to nurture a lively imagination. This leaves an artist with a pretty wide canvas to work on, even on a wet Monday morning. It is true, of course, that we all tend to have special themes and subjects which interest us particularly, and most artists tend eventually to be identified by the subject-matter of their pictures as well as by their individual style, but simply waiting for the Muse to arrive is more likely to bring on haemorrhoids and poverty than brilliant ideas. One of our own most highly acclaimed painters has declared that he seeks inspiration and ideas by visiting book shops which specialise in medical text books and there he seeks out vividly illustrated books on diseases of the mouth. The exciting colours, he says, help him when he is painting his screams. I believe him, but I do not have the stomach for that sort of interest myself and prefer to play about with brightly coloured shipping in the mouth of the River Dart. No criticism of a fellow artist is implied and I mention it only to illustrate the wide variety of subject-matter which may motivate a painter.

Poplar Plantation. Water-colour 14″ × 10″.

My own all-consuming interest is in Britain itself, particularly all that is implied by rural England. That means its rich and widely varied landscape, its farms and villages and infinite wealth of architecture, as well as its trees and flowers, birds and animals of every kind. But more than that, although I grumble as much as the next man about our weather, I love the moods and atmosphere of this country. I am fascinated by mists and scudding clouds, by the gentle breeze that sways the tall poplar or the angry gale that thrashes through the woodlands filling the air with flying leaves like dark snowflakes. I love the pouring rain, too – it is marvellous to paint. Water is just as exciting – in a tumbling mountain stream, a slow meandering river or rough and well-salted crashing against the coast.

There are not many people in my landscape paintings, which implies no lack of interest in human beings; it is simply that they all seem to have crowded into my other Britain where they can be dealt with in more depth. On the rare occasions when I have introduced them into my landscapes they worry me a little. Even when they are in the distance with their backs turned I cannot rid myself of the feeling that they are up to something. I prefer them to go away and leave me in peace to contemplate nature alone. They will all be back on my drawing-board soon enough, causing mayhem of one kind or another, and I do try to give them a nice little bit of old England to fool about in, which proves that I love them really.

The Duke's Head, Timsbury. Water-colour 10¼″ × 14½″.

171

My preference in landscape painting is to work outdoors from beginning to end of the picture, but this is rarely possible for one reason or another. I succeed in doing it sometimes by working from my camper van where I can have all my tools about me and enough food to keep me going for the day. Such days are heaven but there are many snags. It's true that sudden changes in the weather are much less important but it is increasingly difficult to find a view which I want to paint and a place to park my vehicle which allows me to see it properly. All the finest scenery seems to be discernible only from narrow country lanes where even to slow down my vehicle can start a riot of anger and abuse from fellow drivers.

Herons Mead Pool. The long hot summer of 1973. Water-colour 14″ × 9¾″.

On one occasion I settled by eight o'clock in the morning in a delightful glade in the New Forest and started to paint. I swear there was not another human being for miles in any direction. By nine o'clock I had laid in some pretty satisfactory washes and was at peace with the world when a car drew up beside me and came to a halt right in front of my open door, so close that I could have almost touched its side without getting off my stool, thus completely obscuring the view. The doors flew open and a rough-looking character with his wife and four children poured out. The man and his wife ignored me completely but the kids (grasping a brightly coloured football) gathered round the door and said:

'Watcha doin' Mista?'

'Trying to paint the view,' I said.

'You a nartist then Mista?'

'I'm trying to be,' I said.

'Dad! Dad! That man's a nartist. 'E's trying to paint a picture.'

'Well leave 'im alone,' he said. 'I thought you wanted to play football.'

I moved on and tried somewhere else but the nuance of the day had gone. There were two dusty circles on the windscreen and one on the side door where the football had hit it.

Cedar Tree at Wilton House. Water-colour 14″ × 10″.

I recall another lovely summer day on Exmoor. No van this time. I was sitting on a stool perched on a boulder in the little river that flows under the Devil's Bridge in the Doone country. My friend and sketching companion, Ray Evans, was sitting nearby and we had both about half-completed our pictures. The Devil's Bridge is a small hump-backed bridge, very narrow and quite unsuitable for motor vehicles. As the lane in both directions is also very narrow we were surprised to see a coach full of people come along and try to turn onto the bridge. It must have been perfectly obvious to the driver that there was no possible chance of getting onto the bridge and that the banks of the little stream were so steep that it would have been quite hazardous to try crossing it on foot. There was much to-ing and fro-ing and grinding of gears before the driver decided to give up the attempt. He reversed the great bus for about twenty yards, threw it noisily into forward gear and launched it over the edge of the bank. The radiator scattered a few rocks and buried itself into the bottom of the opposite bank, leaving the vehicle at an angle of forty-five degrees and all the passengers convinced that their end had come. The end of our painting session had certainly come but, happily, all the passengers got out more or less unscathed and sat about in disconsolate groups whilst the driver walked off down the lane to find help. He was going to need a very heavy crane.

Painting outdoors is a wonderful experience if you are lucky, but I find that it is usually possible to do only part of the work in the open air and I complete the paintings in my studio. I don't think that it really matters much where or how one works on a picture provided that the result is satisfactory. I find that I can often produce equally good paintings by working entirely from sketchbook drawings and in the comparative comfort of my workroom with all the necessary tools to hand; it is much easier to control the degree of moisture in the paper when I am working towards some special effect or subtlety of technique. It must be said, however, that the lively freshness which is so often the chief delight of a quick sketch is not always easy to recapture in the most carefully considered studio painting.

Welsh Farm. Pencil sketch.

11: TIME TO STAND AND STARE

Frosty Morning at Timsbury, 20 December 1976. Water-colour 12½″ × 9¼″.

Although I was continuing to work for *Punch* and other publications throughout the sixties and seventies, I was finding ever-increasing interest in producing humorous books on a variety of subjects. Like almost everything else I have done, they seemed to develop by accident rather than design and by the time we had settled into our present home I was working on the tenth volume, which dealt with the crazy sort of things we humans do in the name of leisure. There were already books on country life, house-hunting, dogs, angling and gardening, apart from those on riding,

and I had a list of subjects which I was looking forward to working on.

In 1975 Methuen put on a very nice party to celebrate the sale of a million paperbacks, at a time when a minor industry was developing in the merchandising of characters and drawings from my books. I am bound to admit that things were taking on an air of unreality and I found it increasingly difficult to believe that any of it had anything to do with me. There was certainly no possible way I could have controlled or even kept in touch with what seemed to be going on and it was entirely

thanks to Alan Delgado, who had become my close friend as well as my agent, that I was left fairly reasonably free to get on with the only thing I was capable of doing fairly well, which was getting ideas and making pictures. It would be quite untrue to suggest that I did not get a great deal of pleasure from the situation and I quote a particular incident to illustrate the point.

I walked into a bookshop in Salisbury one day and was pleased to see a great pyramid of my latest book on display. I was torn between pleasure at seeing so many copies on sale and the terror which always grips me on such occasions. Whatever will the publisher do with that lot, I asked myself, if nobody buys them?

A customer came along, surveyed the display and opened a copy. It was a terrible moment. Would he sneer and put it down? Would he show signs of interest or amusement and would he . . . would he perhaps . . . buy a copy? He was a lovely man –, his face creased into a broad grin . . . he turned the page and he crumpled forward . . . I could have hugged him. He took out his handkerchief and was dabbing his eyes when he noticed me grinning at him.

'Oh God,' he said, 'have you looked at this book?'

'Well, er . . . yes,' I said, 'as a matter of fact it's my book.'

He glanced at the copy in his hand and then at the pile on the display stand. 'I'm sorry,' he said, looking puzzled. 'You mean this copy's yours?'

'Well no, not exactly. What I mean is that I wrote the book and I'm delighted to see that you like it.'

'You didn't!' he said.

'Honestly,' I said.

'You mean you did these drawings too?'

'Cross my heart and hope to die,' I said.

'Is your name Thelwell?'

'Yes.'

'Well, I'll be . . . would you autograph it for me?'

Moments like that don't happen every day but when they do they're great fun. Particularly if, like the Salisbury gentleman, they buy three copies.

It was really surprising to me how often a series of quite random occurrences seemed to link together to produce interesting work. Hampshire has many delightful pubs and one summer evening when I was leaving the Bear and Ragged Staff, near Kimbridge, with a few friends, I happened to look up at the pub sign. It struck me that the name sounded as if those who worked in the pub went about in very tatty clothes or wore none at all. It was no more than a passing thought and I have always been too lazy and inefficient to carry a notebook in which to record possibly useful ideas. It takes all my concentration to remember my sketchbook.

It was only a few months later that I was invited by Guinness to do their calendar for 1973. Much fine work had been done over the years by artists of great ability for Guinness and I was very sorry to find that it was quite impossible to fit the work in that year. However, I suggested to their publicity director that if they would allow me to leave the work until the next year I would submit a set of ideas to them based on traditional British pub signs. It was the kind of job which occasionally turns out to go without a hitch and is very enjoyable to do. It turned out, also, to become something of a collector's item and Guinness, in addition to the calendar, issued attractive sets of prints which were framed and used as wall decorations in pubs all over the country.

I was particularly amused by the sensitive way in which the Guinness directors reacted to the least suggestion that anyone could be affected by alcohol when consuming their product. They clearly liked the whole idea and the artwork which I submitted to them but they politely suggested that they would be pleased if I would agree to make a slight alteration to two of the designs.

One of them showed a group of people sitting at tables outside a country pub and a man who had just emerged from the door with a tray of drinks had walked smack into the post which held the inn sign 'The Seven Stars'. It was clear that all the man could see were the seven stars which were circling his head. The other subject was 'The Jolly

Huntsman'. This showed a hunt meet with the mounted members politely consuming their stirrup cups and looking horrified at a pink-coated gentleman lying flat on his back under his horrified horse. His legs were sticking up in the air and he had a wide, inebriated grin on his face. 'The Seven Stars' was changed to a man just entering the pub and striking his head on a low beam. 'The Jolly Huntsman' I changed to a gentleman who had left his hunting horn at home and equipped himself instead with an immense tuba which went several times round his body and ended in a huge brass bell over his head. He had a rubber motor-horn bulb on the other end.

I much preferred the original ideas.

The Seven Stars.
The Nag's Head.

Four pub signs from the Guinness calendar.

The Wool Pack.
The Bird in Hand.

Horseracing by
thelwell

We asked Thelwell to design
a horseracing set of stamps.
We reproduce his work here.
Our nerve failed us when it
came to using them as stamps
but they are too good to miss
so we have included them in
the pack.

Printed in England by Moore & Matthes (Printers) Limited

The text of this book is included
in the American bestseller
ALL CREATURES GREAT AND SMALL
'The happiest book of the year'
New York Times

IF ONLY
THEY COULD
TALK
JAMES HERRIOT

*(top) Postage stamp designs for the
GPO.
(above left) Symbol for the Riding for
the Disabled Association.
(above right) Paperback drawing for one
of James Herriot's vet books.
(left) Greetings card design.*

Another series of paintings which I have greatly enjoyed doing also came about by a combination of circumstances. I had admired the old sporting prints and paintings which were so popular in the latter half of the eighteenth and early nineteenth century ever since I first discovered them in library books when I was about thirteen. I had at that time never heard of artists like Pollard, Fernley and Sawrey Gilpin and I was very impressed by the skill and beauty of their work. In the early sixties I had submitted a set of pencil roughs to *Punch* which were based on the old sporting prints but with an added twist of my own. They were not accepted but years later I adapted one of the ideas for a *Punch* front cover and there, as far as I was concerned, the matter would have ended. In about 1970, however, I was invited to produce six paintings for table mats and it occurred to me that the commission might be a good chance to develop the sporting prints theme. Alan Delgado later showed the work to the Tryon Gallery in Dover Street and they published all six pictures as signed limited editions which were so popular that other paintings on the sporting prints theme followed. The work was printed by Royles, who later issued the growing collection as greetings cards and calendars and, like the books, they spread westward to the USA and Canada and eastwards as far as Japan and New Zealand. There were about fifty subjects in the series when Methuen published the first collection in book form in 1984 under the title *Thelwell's Sporting Prints*.

(below) This Christmas card, one of a series produced for Royle Publications Ltd, has proved to be the all-time bestseller throughout the company's long history. Mr Julian Royle tells me that it brought the Santa Claus character back into Christmas cards after a gap of about twenty years.

(right) From Sporting Prints,
and published by the Tryon Gallery,
Dover Street, in a limited edition print.
(above) Rough Shoot; (below) Smooth Shoot.

Ranworth Church from Malthouse Broad, Norfolk. Water-colour 7½″ × 5¼″.

Three Swans at Herons Mead. Sketch 7½″ × 11″.

By 1977 there were seven more books of humour in print including *The Effluent Society*, another volume on property called *This Desirable Plot*, a sailing manual called *Three Sheets in the Wind*, *Penelope* – a riding book in strip cartoon form – *Belt Up*, a manual for motorists, a book on riding for cowboys called *Thelwell Goes West*, and one on bringing up children called *The Brat Race*.

(below) From *Thelwell Goes West*.

Do not get anxious on difficult terrain –
you may communicate your feelings
to your horse.

The cow-hand may be on the trail
for weeks at a time.

THE CALL OF THE SEA

'I should have known when I saw
the self-steering gear.'

Sailing is the fastest growing
participation sport of modern times.

MEN AND THEIR MOTORS

WOMEN AT THE WHEEL

(above) From *Three Sheets in the Wind*.

(below) From *Belt Up*.

'Don't panic, Cynthia, it's gravy!'

Make him his own scratching-post
or he might damage the furniture.

Make him his own cat-door so that he can
get in and out when he wishes.

(above) From *Magnificat.*

(below) From *Gymkhana.*

Examine his legs daily for signs of trouble.

Introduce him to easy jumps
until he gains confidence.

One of the themes which I had pursued over a number of years in *Punch* was the dilemma of the owners of the stately homes of England. I think the reason why the subject was so fascinating to me was that these beautiful great houses with their vast collections of art treasures were created in merry old England by class privilege of such an order that the inequality of human existence could never be defended by logical argument.

Nevertheless, if it had not been for the inequality it is certain that the country as a whole would not have been graced by so many of these beautiful buildings and in one sense at least would have been the poorer for it. Changing social and economic conditions and two world wars had greatly reduced the inequality, however, and had left the landed gentry with properties which were becoming ever more expensive to maintain with

'You rang, Sir?'

From *The Tatler* and *Some Damned Fool's Signed the Rubens Again.*

less and less money to spend on them. The fact that almost all of them had to open their houses to the *hoi polloi* in order to survive somehow brought them down to the point where they could be seen as simple human beings like the rest of us, with problems not unlike our own but on a much larger scale. Once I began to apply the ordinary day-to-day problems of life to the inhabitants of the stately homes a whole new world of comical situations was thrown up – like washday, for example. When her ladyship has to do her own washing did she have to take down all those standards and banners and flags which hung in

serried ranks thirty feet up the wall in the medieval hall? When a family portrait had to be sold to raise money to repair the roof did the noble lord and his lady wife have a slanging match about whose ancestor was to be sacrificed? And how did the nobility tell their teenage sons to get their tatty long hair cut when surrounded by portraits of ancestors sporting huge beards, curling sideboards and mountainous wigs? A series of stately-home drawings appeared in the *Tatler* as well as those in *Punch*, and in 1982 Methuen published a book of them under the title *Some Damn Fool's Signed the Rubens Again.*

From *Punch* and *Some Damned Fool's Signed the Rubens Again.*

'We can never catch the visitors at it, M'lord.'

One might imagine that people would resent being the subject of humorous drawings; but they do not. On the contrary, they are usually the first to ask for the original drawing to frame for their office or lounge wall. This is true of the professions such as doctors and lawyers, scientists, estate agents, churchmen and politicians. Some subjects such as serious illness, physical disabilities and death are taboo as far as most cartoonists are concerned because they feel the object of their work is to entertain and not to wound or cause offence; but there are a few, particularly on the continent, who specialise in black humour and they have a certain minority following.

As my own riding drawings developed they became quite wildly knockabout and children as well as adults were thrown about, tossed through the air and deposited in hedges, ditches and even up trees. I know from personal experience how parents worry about the safety of their children when out riding and it occurred to me that some people might take exception to the hazardous situations I often depicted, but not once in over thirty years has anyone criticised the drawings on this basis. Indeed, I have on a number of occasions been asked by parents to autograph or write a short message in one or other of my riding books to be given to a child who was recovering from a riding accident and I have had several letters claiming that the books were of considerable help in speeding the recovery of an injured child. It is astonishing how tolerant human beings are of human misfortune and how angrily they react if an animal is shown in a similar predicament.

On the whole people are either fond of animals or indifferent to them, but cats seem to bring about an almost fanatical reaction from most of us. It has always been so. The early Egyptians worshipped them as gods whilst in medieval Europe they were believed to be agents of the devil and were treated with cruelty and loathing and even today few people seem to take a neutral attitude towards them. They are either adored or disliked by almost everyone, which may explain why books about cats are almost always popular. I was told as long ago as 1957 that if I wanted to do a humorous book about animals I would be well advised to choose cats and it took me twenty-six years to get round to following that advice. I found that the work went so well that not a single alteration or redrawing occurred throughout the dummy run. I was therefore left with a fully finished set of drawings which I felt would not be improved in any way by drawing them all over again. It was the first time that such a thing had happened and it was very pleasing – but there was a snag. Because it was a dummy book I had drawn on both sides of each page and all the pages were bound together. To say the least, this is not convenient for the publishers or the printers, but it is quite surprising how difficulties can be overcome by skilled craftsmen. The published version of *Magnificat* is in fact an exact facsimile of the original dummy.

My normal method of producing a book has always been to research the subject thoroughly first and to make copious notes of all facts and fantasies connected with the subject gleaned from every available source. This information is then sorted into a number of sections which might make chapters in the finished work and each piece of information carefully considered to see whether it can be treated in a humorous way. If it seems promising it is put onto a second list and the first list is discarded. Books are produced in multiples of 16 or 32 pages and it is normally the publisher's responsibility to organise the typescript so that it fits exactly into the number of pages available. Books of drawings, however, particularly if there is to be a fixed number of drawings on each page, cannot be dealt with in this way and it is vital that the artist knows from the start how many pages are at his disposal so that he can produce the right number and size of drawings to fit the pages.

Chapters in this kind of book read better if they start on a right-hand page so that it is important to have all drawings properly organised to fit both chapter lengths and the length of the book as a whole. I find it simplifies the process to work out the script and drawings in a plain dummy book which has the same overall dimensions as the printed book will have. There can then be no mistakes in organising each page. My next step is to draw the book in its entirety in the dummy volume. In almost all cases there will be alterations to both script and drawings at this stage and only when I am satisfied that all is exactly how I wish it to be are finished drawings made on separate sheets of paper.

One of the questions most frequently put to cartoonists is 'Where do you get your ideas from?' I have never been able to give a satisfactory answer because the truth is that I do not know. I have never been able to discover a formula; I simply muddle along hoping for the best. I have never leapt from the bath shouting 'Eureka!' nor have I been struck with a brilliant idea while shaving. Indeed, my mind scarcely functions at all before 11 a.m. and I am convinced that every time I get an idea it will be my last. I do not recall seeing any real-life situation, however amusing, which was immediately translatable into a satisfactory cartoon. A good idea, when it comes, seems so obvious that I wonder how I could possibly have overlooked it all my life and I feel almost in a panic to turn it into a finished cartoon before the whole world thinks of it and gets in first.

No one can convince another person that an idea or a drawing is funny or that it is not. For, like beauty, visual humour is in the eye of the beholder. As far as I am concerned the best ideas are those that spring from familiar or readily recognisable situations which are carefully taken apart by the artist and rebuilt for maximum speed and impact and timed to perfection. If the familiar aspect can be presented with an unexpected twist, so much the better. The effect is sometimes more potent if the drawing depicts the moments before

From *Punch* and *Thelwell Country*.

the climax of the idea or the moment which follows it. This allows each individual to use a certain amount of imagination when looking at the drawing and gives extra scope for enjoyment.

Although his object in life might be similar, a cartoonist is not necessarily a comedian and his technique is certainly quite different, but success for both is dependent not only on amusing ideas but on 'How you tell 'em'. For all humorists the only criterion of success lies in their ability to amuse other people by making them laugh, or smile inwardly or simply feel a warm sense of enjoyment. The comedian will know instantly whether he is succeeding in his chosen profession but freelance artists must work in lonely isolation and wait much longer for reactions, if they come at all. We send out our work like a bat sends out electrical impulses in the dark and it is the signals which bounce back from the public that tell us where we are. If none come back at least we know where we are not.

It has given me deep pleasure to find that both our children, David and Penny, have developed into excellent artists in their own right. Friends express little surprise at this fact, pointing out that as their mother and father are both artists it is quite natural that they should be artists also, presumably by inheritance.

I am less convinced of the inevitability of passing on family traits in this way, however, for I can trace no artists among my own forebears and I know a number of professional artists whose children show no particular ability in that direction. However that might be, I find it very touching to open a book or magazine and see pages made lively and decorative by my own children.

Their work is as different from each other's as Rhona's is from mine, which makes the whole

Design for a Royle greetings card.

mystery that much more interesting and exciting.

About 1976 I realised that I had been working for *Punch* for more than twenty-five years. I had enjoyed it very much but it seemed a good time to pause and take stock, for there were other avenues I wanted to explore more closely. I wanted to devote more time to painting, for there is nothing in life more enjoyable than painting for the sheer love of it, with no other object in view than the hope of producing something which is inwardly satisfying.

In some ways life is a bit less hectic than it used to be but there are hundreds of sketches and ideas I would like to develop, books I would like to do and pictures I want to paint. One thing is certain: we do not live long enough to do more than scratch the surface of possibilities. This is far from being a tragic situation, for tragedy comes only when one feels that there is nothing left to do.